How to Understand and Petition for

Your Decree of Nullity

D1603779

How to Understand and Petition for

Your Decree of Nullity

A Little Book with BIG Help

Rose Sweet

Saint Benedict Press
Charlotte, North Carolina

ISBN: 978-1-935302-60-5

Cover design by Christopher J. Pelicano

Printed and bound in the United States of America.

Saint Benedict Press
Charlotte, North Carolina
2012

Table of Contents

Part 4: Receiving the Decision

There's No Such Thing as "Catholic Divorce"

DIVORCE—the so-called death of a marriage, of hopes and dreams—continues to increase in what Pope John Paul II coined our "culture of death." But the beauty of our faith is that there is always hope and healing for those who seek it—from Christ, through His Church. Seeking a Decree of Nullity after a civil divorce can produce profound benefits in many ways, as I know firsthand; I went through the humbling but healing process after I found myself divorced. Today I'm privileged to serve in the Diocese of San Bernardino, California, as a lay advocate for those seeking a Decree of Nullity, helping them prove what went on before and during their marriages. It's one of the most meaningful areas of my ministry to those who have been divorced.

An authentic marriage can never be dissolved—hence, there is no such thing as "Catholic divorce," which many people consider an annulment to be. Although the word "annulment" is commonly used—and I use it in this book—it is inaccurate. The proper term is Decree of Nullity (or Declaration of Nullity), which asserts, not that a marriage has ended, but that a valid marriage did not exist from the beginning. A Decree of Nullity is a result of the following:

◇ The Church always presumes the marriage bond was created and addresses validity only if the marriage has definitely failed.

◇ The civil divorce must have already been filed and recorded.

◇ The Church determines if there even was a valid marriage from the start by examining the relationship of the spouses, primarily prior and up to the time they said, "I do."

◇ Marriages don't have to be perfect to be valid. But if what looked like a marital bond never really formed—despite good attempts—then the Church (through the diocesan tribunal) will witness the truth by issuing a Decree of Nullity.

The Church is here to help

Annulments begin at the diocesan level. Many churches under a bishop in a geographical area form a diocese. Each diocese is served by a tribunal, an assembly of those qualified (including judges) to conduct judicial business within the Church, according to canon law (the law of the Church). The procedural language or terminology may vary slightly between dioceses, but what appears in this book is commonly recognized and understood.

The parish priest often serves as the advocate who helps the Petitioner—the one claiming there was no true marriage bond *from the start*—to submit a petition to the tribunal for a Decree of Nullity. The other spouse is called the Respondent. Often lay men and women can also be trained to help parishioners in the annulment process. A cleric may advocate (defend another) for a party in the annulment process, but when it is a lay person who helps, he or she is called a lay advocate.

Terri (our parish wedding coordinator) and I went to advocate training in our diocese together. We became fast friends and decided that we would serve as a lay advocate team, working on each case together. "Two minds are better than one," Terri would tell those who came to the parish office to begin their annulment process.

Terri would explain the forms, and I would take notes and help the person put the petition into writing. Throughout the investigation we'd check and challenge each other to make sure we'd gotten as much information as possible to help determine "grounds"—the basis on which a marriage can be declared null and upon which the petition is submitted. We've heard people pour out deep pain and sorrow—and lots of anger—

about their failed marriages. Some are relieved to be separated, and others are still bitter. More than a few are still in shock and wondering what happened. Sadly, profound suffering always preceded each divorce: abuse, childhood neglect and abandonment, adultery, teenage pregnancies, homosexuality, abortions, drugs, addictions, fears, pressures, and anxieties. We've even heard stories of criminal abduction, murder, and witchcraft. Terri and I try to create a warm, safe place where people can vent, cry, and ask questions about how the Church may be able to declare their marriage null.

From our experiences—and the help of good friends who are canon lawyers or who work in diocesan tribunals—comes this book, which is both a "why" and a "how-to." The Catholic Church's teachings on annulments can't be properly appreciated until one first understands the nature of a valid marriage bond. What I hope the reader will come to understand is that a *valid sacramental marriage is one that is able to share in the nature of, and be caught up into, that passionate, powerful, and perpetual marriage of Jesus Christ and his Bride, the Church.* The Church is all baptized Christians, individually and collectively. We're all called to say yes to God's proposal of eternal communion—a marriage of sorts—with Him. The Church's teachings are about love, romance, and happily-ever-after the way it was always meant to be. And that should give us great hope.

No marriage is perfect!

We're all imperfect and we love imperfectly, so no marriage is perfect. It's a life-long journey and process for a married couple and their relationship to be caught up into God's love, and no one ever does it fully. But an imperfect marriage does not make that marriage invalid.

Many times marriages suffer because people in the marriage sin, and that can cause great hardship on everyone. But sin and struggles in themselves do not invalidate a marriage.

What renders a marriage bond invalid are fatal flaws that must have been present at the time of the wedding. When the marriage fails, only then can the parties— with the help of their pastor, their advocate, and the tribunal—look back to when they said, "I do." Then they can discern what was there (or not there) that ultimately caused the marriage not only to fail but to never fulfill the requirements of the sacrament.

Many times, however, troubles in the relationship are not a sign of invalidity but simply the result of our selfish natures. That's when we need to bear with our spouse and lean on God's grace to get us through the tough times that can make us holier. How often we forget that marriage is less about *happiness* than it is about *holiness*! With God's grace we can learn to be patient and forgiving with our spouse, again and again . . . just as God is with us.

You can understand annulments

This book first addresses the origin of marriage and the "diamond of consent" that makes it valid.

Next, the grounds (reasons) for an invalid consent—which must be present at the wedding—are briefly addressed, *but I make no attempt to compete with other fine books on the market that cite from Church canons in more depth and with study cases.* A basic understanding of grounds is necessary to present an effective petition.

The next section is a comprehensive inventory of the tough questions that will help the Petitioner, the Respondent, and the Witnesses—as well as the advocate—in drawing out the truth and adequately documenting it in the petition for nullity.

Lastly, I address what to do while you wait for a decision from the tribunal and when the decision comes.

Canon law regarding the annulment process is exhaustive—to protect the indissolubility of marriage. Thank God! The gift of marriage as He gave it to us continues to come under great assault. The Church, under the guidance of the Holy Spirit, must protect it. But this book is in no way meant to cover everything, and I try to avoid too much technical jargon. It's a general overview for those who might be called to be part of the annulment process and for those who minister to them. For more detailed questions and some interesting case studies, I recommend these books written by competent canon lawyers with many years of experience working in tribunals:

> *Annulments and the Catholic Church: Straight Answers to Tough Questions,* by Edward Peters, J.D., J.C.D. (Westchester, Pennsylvania: Ascension Press, 2004).

> *Annulment: The Wedding That Was: How the Church Can Declare a Marriage Null,* by Michael Smith Foster (Mahwah, New Jersey: Paulist Press, 1999).

Part 1

Understanding Marriage

Chapter 1

The Church Is Our Mother

THE first question some might have is: *How can the Church tell us whether our marriage was valid or not?*

The annulment process (or rather, seeking a Decree of Nullity) is one of the most misunderstood processes in the Catholic Church. To help our understanding, let's first consider two important points:

1.) It is the couple who—by their free, informed, and able consent, expressed as "I do"—confer the sacrament of marriage on each other. The Church minister does not marry them; they marry each other. The minister officiates as a witness to their act.

2.) When a marriage is declared to be invalid, it is not the Church who makes it null. Again, the Church acts as the public witness to what *the couple* did, or did not do, that invalidated the sacrament.

This serious claim affects not just you and your ex-spouse but the whole Mystical Body of Christ and, in a way, all of society. Marriage—if valid—is an unbreakable bond that is the very foundation of the human family and church community. It must be revered and protected, and its sanctity upheld. So, just as the Supreme Court represents everyone in our country in determining questions of law, the tribunal takes care of these matters in the name of the whole church.

Canon law is the basis of each case. These are the norms that govern the practice of Catholics around the world. They are called the universal laws of the Church.

When the validity of a marriage is questioned, it's the Church tribunal that says, "We have been given authority to help you. Let us assist in the investigation of your marriage so that Truth may be upheld." The tribunal is not a cast of old, celibate men who want to make everyone miserable; it is a trained team of clergy and laity who've been called to help bring healing to divorced families. They are part of the Church, too, and we have to remember that *the Church is our Mother.* She knows that when a marriage fails, there is a broken home and many broken hearts, and as *keeper of our hearts*, she tenderly and compassionately moves in to help. But she's also *keeper of the home* and understands that there are important principles and timeless truths that must be upheld—for the good of the individuals and the whole family of God. She has been given the task by Our Lord to dispense both justice *and* mercy at the same time: a delicate and difficult task for anyone who is not God.

My own mother was the figure of the Church in our family when I was growing up. While she had her own natural authority over me as her child, she also carried my father's full authority over me through her marriage to him. They were "one." He made sure my mother had a set of keys to his car, that she could sign her name on his checks, and that she could charge on his accounts. Because she stayed close to his heart and knew his desires for their children, she ran our household in a way that would honor him and the principles they shared. She was pretty good at dispensing justice, if you know what I mean: the flyswatter did double duty in our home. Mom and Dad knew they had been given their authority over us children by God Himself, and they took their responsibility seriously. They loved us dearly, poured out affection on us regularly, and held us to high moral standards. That's what our spiritual Mother, the Church, does as guardian over her children.

I remember once getting into a heated argument with my younger sister, Serena, when I was about twelve years old. We had been given the same kind of doll for the previous Christmas; Serena's had white yarn braids, and mine had pink. I had cared lovingly for my doll, propping her up on my pillows each morning and making sure she was clean and neat. But Serena didn't care for her doll as well as I did mine.

One day after a spring rain, I saw our family dog—an Australian Shepherd named Lassie—shaking something wet and muddy in her mouth. I ran over to see what it was and was aghast to discover the hardly recognizable rag was Serena's doll! I rescued the doll from Lassie, ran into the house, took off the doll's little dress, washed her cloth body, shampooed and re-braided her hair, and tried my best to make her look new again. After several hours of primping and fluffing, she was clean and dry, and I placed her on my pillow next to my doll. They looked like little sisters!

Months went by, and it was apparent Serena didn't even miss her doll. But one day she came into my bedroom, saw her doll, and went over to snatch it off the bed. "Hey!" I yelled. "That's MY doll now!"

"No, it isn't. It's *mine!*"

"You left it outside, and Lassie almost ate it! Give it back right now!"

"NO! I'm going to tell MOM!"

Whenever Serena was about to lose an argument, she'd run and tattle to our mother. But I was ready.

"No, I'LL tell Mom!" I yelled. "I'll tell her *everything!*" I pushed past Serena, shoving her into the wall, and running to get to Mom first.

I should have been an attorney. The two of us stood before Mom like courtroom adversaries. Mom was the judge, and I knew I had to present a convincing case in order to win. So I started at the beginning and told

Mom how I had rescued the poor, *sweet* little doll that had no one to love her; how I had practically rescued her from certain death by the dog, made a safe home for her in my room, and that justice demanded that I now have ownership of the doll. I waited confidently for the verdict to be in my favor. What happened next taught me a very valuable lesson in life. Mom looked at me with the deepest compassion and tenderness.

"Honey," she said, "that was very thoughtful and loving of you to rescue the doll. You've got the heart of a very good little mother." I beamed, but my smile faded with Mom's next words.

"I know you've become attached to the doll . . . but she belongs to Serena."

WHA-A-A-AT! I thought. *No fair!* "But, Mom . . ." I begged.

She took the doll gently out of my arms and gave her to Serena, who had a smug smile on her bratty little face. Ugh-h-h! I could hardly stand the injustice of it all!

Mom put her arm around me, gave me a squeeze, and lovingly said, "Honey, I want you to remember something. You can't just take people's belongings because they don't care for them as you would. As unfair as that seems, the right thing to do is to protect what belongs to others. And that's a family rule that someday will protect you, too. Remember when *you* left your bike out in the rain? What would you have done if Serena had taken it, dried it off, and started riding it?"

I knew Mom was right. I guess I even knew it way back when I pulled the doll out of the mud and decided to take possession of it. I had simply hoped that my good intentions and diligent efforts could change the truth. We are all susceptible to falling into that way of thinking or hoping sometimes, especially if we think we were the "good one" in our marriages.

Marriage is not just a private matter. In both the Church and the state, it has a public/social dimension as well. What went on between Serena and me could have had larger implications for all my siblings, especially if we could all start taking each other's toys and claiming them as our own. Human persons are not isolated or free to do what they want when they want. Family, state, and church—the world—would be in chaos.

In the annulment process both sides get to tell their story if they wish. The Church tribunal listens, as my mom had listened carefully to both sides. Mom had to uphold the higher principle, but she also showed me every bit of compassion and understanding she could— mother to child. She gently explained the principles so I could move past the disappointment and grow in wisdom. Mom loved me enough to know that there were more important things for me to possess than just a doll: kindness, understanding, patience, and long-suffering. Mom's desire for me was not that I get everything I wanted in my immaturity, but that I possess the virtues that would make me holy and happy, even though she knew it might hurt.

"Thank you," to Holy Mother Church—and to all the men and women who work in the annulment process, who act as my mother did. They consider the minds and hearts of the couple, and still uphold the indissolubility of marriage and the greater good for all. Many times we're simply like young children who don't understand marriage, divorce, annulments, and a lot of other Church teachings. In a world where everyone acts as he or she pleases, there would be utter chaos. The law—and all the forms it takes—is meant to guard and protect the rights and dignity of all human persons. Church law is the same, calling Christians to a higher way of seeing the world and living in it.

So start from the beginning, and take a chapter at a time. I'm so sorry that you had to go through divorce. You're part of a big family who wants to guide you through the process of healing and give you hope for the future. You are not alone, and your family, the Church, is here to help.

Chapter 2

Everything Is about God

I USED to think everything was about me.

When I couldn't get what I wanted, I went to God as if He were the Divine Vending Machine; I inserted prayers, Masses, novenas, and rosaries as if they were quarters, nickels, and dimes. I pushed the "I promise to be good" button and waited for my dreams to come popping out. Not.

It wasn't until I had been divorced—more than once—and was facing a life of many failures that I meekly called out to God for real help. "I don't need the things You can give me . . . I need YOU. But I'm scared. Help me." That open door in my humbled heart was all the space needed for the Holy Spirit to swoosh in and begin cleaning house. Oh, the demolition process and rebuilding—including annulment—has been painful! But fruitful!

I finally faced the truth I had always known: *that no human person, place, or thing can ever satisfy the deepest needs and cries of my heart.* Not even marriage. Everything is about God. He is good, true, and beautiful, and everything in the created world that is good, true, and beautiful is a pale reflection of Him. Like a Bridegroom who woos his betrothed with a flashing, fiery stone in a setting of pure gold, God woos us—His Bride—with the gift of all the gorgeous and mysterious creation.

What does this have to do with annulments? Everything. Keep reading.

Everything points to and brings us to God

One day after my divorce, I prayed to God, "I want romance. I want to be in love. I want kids. It's almost been like an obsession. Even after the pain of divorce, I STILL WANT IT ALL! Arghh-h-h! What's wrong with me? *Why* did You make me this way, God?"

Thankfully, I shut up and was quiet long enough to listen and hear Him answer. As if He spoke to my thoughts, I heard, "Oh, Rose, don't you know that I AM the Love you seek?" I stayed still and kept listening.

"I designed everything in the created order to point you to me—*including romance and marriage*. All these things will pass away, but my love for you never will. Look deep into your desires for love, romance, and fairytales . . . and you will find ME."

That was the beginning of my discovery of the *real* meaning of marriage. And once I properly understood marriage, I understood annulment. I hope you will too.

God is Love

God has revealed Himself to be Three Divine Persons who are united in—and are constantly exchanging—perfect love. In a sense, they form a Divine Family. Their love spills out to us, gives us life, and invites us in that love forever. God is a loving Being who is the endless source of all we desire.

So understanding the true nature of what we call love is central to fully understanding marriage, divorce, and how the Church can declare marriage vows "null." God came to us in the Person of His Son to show us *how* to love the right way, not our way. Jesus reveals that authentic love—the kind that endures—is not just fluffy, feminine romance or hot, passionate sex, although those can be delightful expressions of it. *Love is the hard work of self-emptying and going to the Cross for the good of the other.*

If the couple who stood at the altar and said, "I do" really could not or would not love as God loves humanity, or Jesus loves His Bride—the Church—then their vows may be invalid and their marriage may be only an attempt.

Love is never selfish; it's self-giving

Two people who say, "I do" must know what they are saying for their vows to be valid. Many simply don't know because they have never thought about it deeply enough.

The nature of love is to be a sincere and generous gift to another, but our fallen tendency is to please ourselves. Gross selfishness can take many forms (immaturity, fear, addictions) and can invalidate a couple's attempt to marry.

True love cannot be contained, hidden, capped, bottled, or stopped. Like the Love of God, it pours itself out freely and generously on others for their greater good, even if it means risk, pain, suffering, or death. When we see Jesus on the Cross—dying for His Bride, the Church—we see true love.

Sadly, the fallen nature of man and woman is sometimes painfully present at a wedding. If a bride or a groom has said, "I do" but really meant, "I do . . . *as long as I get what I want*," or "*as long as it doesn't put me at great risk*," or "*until someone better comes along*," then they have put conditions on their love—failing to be fully generous with it—and that makes consent (their exchange of vows) invalid.

Promising to love only for a while (against permanence), under certain conditions (against fullness), with no intent to face great difficulty (reserving the option to run!) is no true promise to love. That counterfeit promise invalidates authentic marriage.

Love invites us into a holy communion

I always thought communion was the part of the Mass where we went up to receive the Consecrated

Host. For many Catholics, the term "Holy Communion" has been understood only as the Eucharist. But I hope by reading here, you will discover much more about the term, since it has a direct bearing on marriage.

"Communion" refers to at least two persons who are closely united in some way. They share a common unity, be it a belief system, a set of values, or a life together. A husband and wife form a communion; their family forms a larger communion of persons, and many more families form communities. But all of these beautiful and loving communions are pale reflections of the most perfect communion: the loving union of the Holy Trinity, the ultimate "Holy Communion (of Persons)."

The highest form of communion that man can enter into is communion with God. Every person was created to spend eternity in sweet, loving union with God, and in the Eucharist we get a taste of what we will have in Heaven forever—real spiritual and bodily communion with God.

God is a loving communion of Persons—a divine "community/family" of sorts.

God invites us to live in that same loving, holy communion now and in Heaven forever.

He gave us *earthly* marriage as a little taste of the *heavenly* marriage.

In marriage, husband and wife must (a) *consent* and (b) *be able* to love as God loves—to experience and enjoy a similar holy communion, *a true marriage.*

Chapter 3

God Is "Husband"; Jesus Is "Bridegroom"

BRIDES and grooms—all of us—are meant to be part of that much bigger, heavenly "marriage."

God gave mankind the spousal analogy when He told the Israelites that they were like an unfaithful bride to Him, their Divine Husband. Then God's people—who certainly understood husband-and-wife relationships—began to see that marriage pointed to something bigger. Jesus told His disciples He was the Bridegroom and that Heaven would be an eternal wedding feast. This tells us that earthly marriage has a much more mystical meaning than we realize!

God wants to "marry" us

In this powerful analogy, God always and everywhere proposes "marriage" to the human soul, inviting us into communion with Him, making us His, and filling us with divine love and life. Completely and forever. In a certain sense, God also wants to "impregnate" the soul with His divine life so we can bear it forth to the rest of the world. Whoa! *Stop and think about that.*

This is not just a romantic image—it's the basis of what makes a sacramental marriage in the Catholic Church. God freely and completely gives us Himself in this "marriage" to us. If either the bride or the groom (or both) did not have a similar *intent* and *ability* to give that freely or fully, then there was not a true marriage bond. We tried—or maybe someone did not try—but many times we just did not know.

To be valid, our earthly marriages must model this divine marriage between God and the human soul, or at least we must be sufficiently free, mature, and able to model it. This spousal analogy helps us to understand what factors must be present to make a valid earthly marriage.

The spousal analogy

God is the Divine "Husband" of all mankind

◇ As a bridegroom pursues his beloved, *God pursues our hearts.*

◇ As the bridegroom prepares a beautiful home for his bride, *God has prepared a place for us (Heaven).*

◇ As a bridegroom tenderly waits and woos, *God gives us room to come to him freely.*

◇ As a bridegroom gives everything he has

and holds nothing back from his bride, *God
gives us fully of Himself.*

◇ As the bridegroom would die before betraying his bride in any way, *God's Love is completely faithful.*

◇ As a bridegroom has the "seed" of life, so
God wants to give us divine life—forever.

We are the bride.

◇ As a bride freely surrenders her whole heart
to her husband, *the human soul freely offers
her life to God.*

◇ As a bride says, "Take all of me; I am yours,"
*the human soul should hold nothing back from
God, loving Him fully.*

◇ As the bride would never give her love to
any other, *the human souls' first love should be
God.*

◇ As a bride freely opens to receive the "seed"
of life, *the human soul opens fully to receive
divine life.*

◇ As a bride carries the divine life in her
womb, *we carry His divine life in our hearts.*

When a husband and wife pledge their love to
each other, their promise (consent) must follow a form
that reflects this same way Jesus loves His Bride: freely,
fully, faithfully, and fruitfully. If we desire and are able
to make this kind of commitment, our marriage gets

caught up into the Divine Marriage, participates in it, and enjoys the abundant graces that flow from it.

If not, the Church can declare that no true marriage was established.

Chapter 4

Consent Makes the Marriage

Our instructor shifted his weight, turned the page on the large book he had placed on his podium, and looked up at his class.

"Let's talk about the 'Diamond of Consent.'"

Diamonds? Our ears perked up. Terri and I were sitting on hard folding chairs in our advocate-training classroom, trying to concentrate on big words like *ex parte intellectus*. We listened intently as our instructor told the class that diamonds are the perfect jewel to represent marriage.

"Consent—as we've learned—is when the couples minister the sacrament to each other by their intent (act of the will). Then they express that consent by saying, "I do." Consent is what makes the marriage. *The valid marriage bond is created, or not, at that moment.* But those words have a who, what, when, where, and why that will make consent valid or invalid. Just as diamonds are multifaceted, there are many 'sides' to consent."

We liked that. As I continued to think about the

diamond analogy, I applied it to the complex theology and church law we had been learning. They, too, have a jewel-like quality with an easy side that reflects truth just as beautifully as the more complex cuts.

Galileo said, "All truths are easy to understand once they are discovered; the point is to discover them." So here is an easy way to remember the TRUTH of valid consent.

The Diamond of Consent

The consent (what) of the couple . . .
Legitimately manifested (where, when, how) . . .
By a bride and groom qualified by the law (who).

And, like the four Cs of a diamond (color, cut, clarity, and carat) valid marital consent has the Four Fs. These qualities of consent reflect the mystical "I do" that Christ the Bridegroom pledges to His Bride, the Church.

Consent must be FREE

God never imposes . . . he *proposes*.

The truth of God's love for us is that we are always FREE to say no to Him. But that's a really bad idea. If the bride or the groom, or both, are compelled by any grave fear or pressure to marry, they are not truly free to say no, and thus their yes loses meaning. Their consent is thus not one that reflects the freedom God gives us, and it is invalid.

Consent must be FULL

"Full" means *in all areas* and *for all time* (until death). Consent cannot be partial. None of us completely rejects God, but there are parts of Him we might not want. Another bad idea. In the sense of giving or receiving only part of someone—and not all of that person—you might say that some people enter marriage with only part of their heart: they want the joys, fun, pleasure, and security of marriage, but not the difficulties or the struggles. They put conditions on their love and leave themselves an escape, such as the option of divorce. This "contraceptive" kind of union is partial at best and invalidates "consent."

Consent must be FAITHFUL

Most people intend to be faithful, but some don't. There are many forms of infidelity in marriage. Sometimes at a wedding, the bride or the groom will think, "If things get really bad, if he or she cheats on me, then it's over. Goodbye. I'm not signing up for *that*!" And since that way of thinking can never reflect the for-better-or-worse "marriage" God has with us, it is not a true marriage. Consent becomes invalid.

Consent must be FRUITFUL

God is love and life. The two cannot be separated. But that is what we do when we refuse to be open to children in marriage. Deliberate contraception in the marital act is an image of the bridal soul saying to Husband God, "I don't want all of you, at least not right now." Another bad idea. To reject God in any way is to reject life. That brings death to the soul and into the marriage.

God never told us we had to have an endless number of children, and neither does His Church. What the Church does teach, however, is that each couple must consider the size of their family *prayerfully* and *unselfishly*. If for a very serious reason (severe depression, illness, or financial hardship, for instance) the couple postpones having children, they must still ensure that their love-making is open to life. How? Not with contraception, which separates life and love, but with waiting to express sexual love when the woman is not in the few fertile days of her monthly cycle. Abstinence.

This continues to be a hot-button issue with Catholics, primarily because of a lack of education, a lack of understanding, and/or an unwillingness to use self-restraint. In our on-demand culture, people often struggle with having to wait a few days if they are trying to postpone having children for a good and unselfish reason. But that's where God's powerful graces can come in and help. If you want to know more about this, go to www.onemoresoul.com

Contraception is sinful, as it separates life from love, but it does not invalidate consent. If, however, either party enters marriage with a firm and absolute refusal ever to be open to children, consent is not only invalid consent; it is *no consent.*

Consent brings about the Sacrament

We were made to be connected with God in every way possible.

Until we get to Heaven—where we'll have perfect communion with God and everyone else who made it there—we can have intimate, special encounters with God through the Sacraments. And because we are spiritual and physical, our connection to God in the Sacraments also has a *spiritual* and a *physical* dimension.

Marriage bridges and unites the invisible world with the visible world, grafting—in a sense—the marrying couple into the marriage of Jesus and His Church. The *physical* part of the sacrament is a visible, tangible, auditory sign—something we can see, touch, and hear—and the *spiritual* part is the invisible reality that corresponds with it. The Church calls the spiritual part the *form* (the right words that reflect the spiritual reality) and the physical part the *matter* (the person, thing, or action through which it happens).

But if the proper *form* (free, full, faithful, and fruitful consent) or *matter* (one man, one woman, both adults, and free to marry) are not present . . . *nothing happens.*

Here's a simple example:

The sacrament of baptism uses (visible) water to

(invisibly) cleanse the soul. The unchangeable characteristics of water are that *it cleanses* and *gives life*. Baptism *cleanses* us spiritually (by washing away Original Sin), and by the graces that flow from it, we are raised to *new spiritual life*. In every sacrament *we "share" in Jesus' death, His victory over sin, and His Resurrection*.

But the water itself doesn't do the trick. We have to say words that reveal our right intent, our free act of the will, and our full faith and trust that God will come into the act and cleanse the soul. We invoke the Holy Spirit with our *words* (form) and using the physical, outward *sign* of cleansing, life-sustaining water (matter). When that happens, you might say the water is now invisibly "charged" with God's power to effect spiritual cleansing.

But what would happen if Father O'Malley used tomato juice instead of water to baptize your newborn son or daughter? Nothing. The outward sign in a sacrament—the person, act, or thing—must be able to accurately and correctly *represent* what is going on. Tomato juice is not a cleansing agent. There has to be consistency and integrity in the "marriage" of the visible signs and the invisible reality.

Okay. So, what would happen if Father used water, but his words were not consistent with inviting the Father, the Son, and the Holy Spirit into the cleansing, life-giving act—such as, "I baptize you in the name of the Church"? Same effect as with tomato juice: *nothing*.

Because words have meaning. They matter.

Words have the power of life and death in them. Baptism must invoke God, who revealed Himself to be Father, Son, and Holy Spirit. The words "the Church" (or other words) do not properly identify God.

You might call this type of ritual an attempted baptism. In this ceremony, hopes were high, water was poured, and words were said, but in the invisible realm, *nothing happened.* No effect. No sacrament.

That's why people of the same sex cannot "marry" each other, as much as they feel they love each other. The visible "signs" of marriage—the human persons of one male and one female—must reflect the permanent, life-giving union of Jesus and His Bride. Our gender has great physical meaning and spiritual significance. Our human matter *matters.* There is a spiritual as well as a physical "sterility" in two so-called grooms or two brides.

Now we're ready to examine these truths in the sacrament of marriage. We'll see how sometimes "hopes were high . . . and words were said," but in the invisible realm there was no spiritual effect.

Because form and matter *matter.*

Part 2

Proving Nullity

Chapter 5

Impediments Nullify Consent

What's wrong with this picture?

CHARLIE is thirteen, but he wants to drive. So his indulgent mother—she never says no to Charlie—takes him down to the Motor Vehicle Department and lies about his age. Her friend works behind the counter and overlooks the obvious when Charlie signs the application. His feet reach the pedals, but Charlie is slow for his age and has trouble reading. "He's such a good boy," his mother tells her friends. They all nod in agreement because Charlie *is* a good boy.

So the state issues Charlie a driver's license and declares him physically and mentally capable of operating a three-thousand-pound machine that could kill him or someone else if he fails to operate it properly. But just because Charlie wanted to, his mother went along, and the state said so, does Charlie really hold a valid driver's license?

Yes and no.

Until proven otherwise, the license is assumed to

be valid. Charlie's attempt to be a good driver is sincere. But he was not of the legal age, nor did he have the maturity to read road signs, follow directions, and make wise decisions. The day Charlie gets arrested and hauled down to juvenile court (along with his mother!) an investigation will take place and his license will be declared null and void. Something similar happens in the annulment process.

People who marry often have the best intent and the support of family. The state will issue them a marriage license. But when the church tribunal begins to investigate their state of mind, maturity, and other factors, they might discover a number of impediments to the *intent* or the *ability* of one or both persons to validly say, "I do" to a *full, free, faithful*, and *fruitful* marriage. No shame, just fact.

A flock of swallows

Imagine a man who boasts at his bachelor party that he has no intention of staying faithful to his bride. Sadly, in some cultures this is very common. His refusal to remain *faithful* automatically invalidates the "I do" he says the next day. A young woman who is pregnant, afraid of public shame, and pressured by her parents to marry is not likely to give marital consent that is *free*. These are clear causes for invalid consent that can usually be clearly supported.

But many times the grounds for declaring consent invalid must arise from what I call "a flock of swallows" (from the saying "A single swallow does not a summer make"). There might not seem to be any single underlying cause for the marital consent to be declared null. *The bulk of many types of evidence will have to point to the grounds.* That's where the Petitioner and the advocate need to dig deep and document thoroughly.

The following are some of the more obvious grounds that may support invalidity. As you read them, mark those that apply to you or to your ex-spouse. Then, when you get ready to prepare your petition, you and your advocate can make sure to tell the story and include the facts.

If one of you is not old enough (Age)

You need to be old enough to know what you are doing when you make vows; otherwise no one can hold you to that promise.

- ◇ According to canon law, a man has to have just turned sixteen (16). A woman has to have just turned fourteen (14).
- ◇ In this category, no particular level of psychological maturity is assumed.
- ◇ For a grave reason involving the public good, the local bishop or one to whom he gives authority could give a dispensation.

If one of you can't have sexual intercourse

Marriage as established by God is ordered to *the openness to* procreation of children. It requires one man and one woman who are capable of expressing their love through sexual intercourse, since this act is a supreme image of the life-giving love of God (husband) in union with the open, receptive human soul (bride).

◇ Permanent impotence that existed prior to the wedding automatically nullifies the marriage.

◇ It can be absolute impotence (with anyone) or relative (in relation to that particular person) and can be on the part of the male or female.

Natural sterility is not the same as impotence. It's sad when a couple can't have children, but their love-making can still be the *free, full, faithful* exchange of love, and the emotional and spiritual *fruitfulness* that comes from their love can be abundant.

If you have a prior marriage (Ligamen)

Anyone who was married can't marry again until that prior marriage is legitimately dissolved or nullified. Remember, *whenever a man and woman say, "I do," the Church presumes that marriage is valid . . . until proven otherwise*. Even if one of you has a civil divorce, for example, but failed to get a Church annulment, that marriage is still assumed to be valid. It's like wanting to sell your car to someone but you never got the title from the former owner. The DMV does not and never has recognized you as the owner of the car. Before you can complete the sale, you have to clear up the ownership title. Annulment is not just legal mumbo-jumbo; it's meant to uphold marriage and the rights and dignity of the persons involved, and to protect the order and civility of the law, which is for the public good.

◇ Anytime one of you said, "I do," a valid bond is presumed to have been created.

◇ The marriage bond can be between the baptized (a sacramental bond) or unbaptized (a natural bond).

◇ Since *consent makes the marriage*, consummation is not necessary for the prior marriage to be considered valid.

◇ For multiple marriages, each must be evaluated separately.

If a Catholic marries an unbaptized person (Disparity of Cult)

Catholics are expected to be "equally yoked": living their faith, understanding its importance, being married to another Catholic or, with the permission of their bishop, another baptized Christian, and living out a sacramental marriage. That's the ideal.

But in reality, Catholics fall in love with and marry non-Christians who have never been baptized. If the bishop grants a Catholic and non-Christian a dispensation, they will have a "good and natural" marriage that is valid but non-sacramental. This means God will be present in their marriage, but they will not be able to access the fullness of graces that come with a sacramental union. However, if they don't get the bishop's permission—and the Catholic hasn't formally renounced the Catholic faith—their "attempted marriage" is not valid.

The bishop may grant permission or a dispensation, securing a promise made by the Catholic to baptize and raise any children in the faith. The non-Catholic should not stand in his or her way.

If one of you is a priest or religious (Holy Orders / Perpetual Vows)

In other times and cultures, married men were and are ordained priests. For instance, we know that the apostle Peter—our first Pope—was married. Today there are many rites within the Church, such as Roman and Eastern, and in the Eastern rites, Catholic priests may be married. However, while in some times and rites, married men can subsequently be ordained priests, once a man is *already ordained*, he is not free to marry. In Ordination a man gives himself totally to the Lord and His Church and is marked as a priest forever. A man who has made this beautiful gift of self and been set apart as a priest or religious is not free to make a second gift of self through marriage. The same is true of a nun or woman religious who has given herself to the Lord through perpetual vows.

For this reason, Holy Orders and perpetual vows are an impediment to marriage. In some cases, the Pope may dispense this impediment if the priest or religious seeks to leave active ministry or the religious life. But without a special papal dispensation, marriage by a priest or religious who has taken perpetual vows is invalid.

If one of you was kidnapped

No valid marriage can exist between a woman and her abductor (the Church assumes the woman was the one kidnapped) unless she chooses him freely and without any fear after she has been separated from him and in a safe place.

◇ Fear and force prevent the consent from being truly free.
◇ This may apply in a highly pressured elopement.

Murder

If a person murders a former spouse in order to marry someone else, even if another person is hired to do the killing, the subsequent marriage is invalid. Sadly, although this sounds like the stuff of movies, it does happen.

Blood relations/affinity

This is a complex issue, and one that gets more complex with the increase in our culture of "blended families." It gets even stickier with the rise of live-in boyfriends or stepparents. "Blood relations" means your natural family. Marriage is not permitted between first cousins or closer.

"Affinity" denotes a relationship by marriage, such as a stepfather or a stepsister. If a young girl grew up in a home with her stepfather, regarding him as a parent and establishing many years of such a relationship, the Church might view their later marriage as invalid. However, imagine a young adult woman who meets, for the first time, the man her mother had married briefly before succumbing to cancer. If the daughter and her mother's former husband subsequently fell in love and married, the Church might find reason to grant a dispensation so they could marry.

The advocate should look for any such relationship, by blood, marriage, adoption, or even living together, including the children of such relationships.

Great compassion and understanding are necessary from the Church in all these cases. We're a wounded culture under constant attack. Lord, have mercy!

Chapter 6

Some Can't or Won't Give Valid Consent

MATT really wants to go to college, but he just doesn't have the grades. He can't pass the exams; not only that: he can't afford it.

Pat wants to join the Marines, but he has an old football injury and some vision problems. He has been rejected.

Audrey wants a car loan, but she's young and hasn't built up her credit score yet. The bank turned her down.

Think about this: in preparing for marriage—the most important relationship we'll ever have and one with the most potential responsibility—none of us has to take a course, score high on an exam, pass a physical, or financially qualify. And worse, we can have mental disorders, emotional problems, addictions—or, as you've just read—a history of abuse, violence and even murder—and still get married.

Matt, Pat, and Audrey are good people with good desires, but they were incapable of achieving the end they wanted. Maybe not forever, but now. In the annulment process, a search is made to see if one or both of the parties were mentally incapable of fulfilling and living out a marriage that was *free, full, faithful,* and *fruitful*—despite how eagerly they wanted it.

This chapter covers both the intent and the ability of the parties to give matrimonial consent.

Grave lack of mental competence

If a person can't think clearly or maturely—mental incompetence—he or she can't give free or full consent. This is why people with severe forms of mental retardation can't marry. This category includes those who are insane and those who lack reason; people who have a history of mental illness might also be included.

Grave lack of judgment (Defect of Discretion)

If a person has gravely flawed judgment or the inability to think things through, and make a wise decision, he or she might not be able to give matrimonial consent. Marriage for a lifetime is serious business. Despite being high-functioning people who drive cars and hold jobs, some people really don't have the mental or emotional ability to give sufficient consideration to this choice. Lots of factors play into this, and each of these should be explored:

◇ The person may have been raised in a family where divorce was common and thought to be an option if things didn't work out.

◇ Young age may be part of the flawed judgment.

◇ The defect of discretion must be very serious, not just "irresponsible."

◇ The person may have ignored many warnings from others.

◇ The decision to marry may have been made quickly—without sufficient thought.

◇ There may have been a strong desire to get out from under the control of overly dominating or abusive parents.

◇ It may have been assumed that once you have sex with someone, you marry that person.

◇ Early problems and regret can signal the lack of judgment.

◇ General pressures (fears) such as pregnancy, peer pressure, fear of being gay, competing with friends or siblings (everyone else is married), getting too old for children, or harsh conditions at home (alcoholic or abusive conditions) may all contribute to an impulsive decision.

Grave lack of competence (incapacity to assume the obligations of marriage for psychological reasons)

This is when one or both of the parties have a serious inability or capacity to live out marriage (that is, assume the essential obligations of marriage) due to psychological causes. They must be able to *understand, agree, enter into,* and *live out* a marriage that is:

Perpetual—Marriage lasts until the natural death of one of the parties.

Indissoluble—There can be no reservation for divorce if it "doesn't work out." Remember that God never leaves us, and marriage is supposed to be an image of—and move us more deeply into—His marriage to us.

Exclusive—No other person should receive the love that is due to a spouse alone. In the spousal analogy with God as our Husband, we as the bride give no one else that primary love. No one.

Faithful—This is not just romantic or sexual faithfulness, but an understanding of what is best for the other person in all areas and a willingness and ability to sacrifice for it. The greatest good of the spouses is their growing holiness.

United—In all areas of the marriage, neither spouse deliberately denies or excludes the other, or withholds anything from him or her. The two are to become "one flesh."

Equal—The obligations, rights, and goods of the union apply equally to both spouses. Marriage is a partnership that is "radically equal."

Open to the gift of children—There can be no permanent refusal to accept the gift of children. An absolute exclusion of children invalidates consent. A love that images God's—and gets caught up into it—must be open to life.

When a married person can't live this way, he or she is not in a valid marriage. What psychological causes can prevent someone from a valid marriage?

- A very weak, passive personality that is easily dominated.
- Psychological problems such as personality disorders (like narcissism), anxiety disorders, long-term depression, alcohol and drug dependencies, schizophrenia, or other conditions categorized in the Diagnostic and Statistical Manual of Mental Disorders, Fourth Edition (DSM IV).
- Fetishes and other odd behavior that may seem harmless should be explored and may point to other deeper issues.
- An addiction to pornography and masturbation can be a substantial deprivation of the goods of marriage to the other spouse.

- ◇ Sex addiction, which makes it difficult to assume the essential obligations of marriage.
- ◇ Practicing a same-sex lifestyle makes it impossible for a person to enter into an exclusively heterosexual marriage. Homosexual tendencies may be an impediment depending on the degree and other factors.

Get professional psychological or psychiatric help with these if the tribunal does not call in its own expert(s).

These conditions must have been present before the wedding.

They must be the cause of the defective consent.

The condition must be permanent, unless treated. If treatable, the marriage may be valid, but that may depend on other factors.

Ignorance

For valid matrimonial consent to exist, the parties must be at least aware of these three facts about marriage: (1) it is only between one man and one woman; (2) it is a permanent union; and (3) it is ordered toward having children by means of some sexual cooperation.

The Church presumes that after puberty, there is no such ignorance. But in some cases—and cultures—this may not be the case. In other words, you have to know where babies come from!

Fraud

If someone lies or withholds something significant from the other—so that they don't have the full truth upon which to base their freely given "I do"—it renders the marital consent invalid. It includes a person's withholding of important information that, if known, would have caused the other person not to have married him or her. It also has to be a quality that would be seriously disturbing to the marriage, not just a bad habit. The deception must have been made in order to get the other person to marry. People might hide such things as:

- ◇ a drug, alcohol, or other serious addiction (gambling, pornography, etc.)
- ◇ having had an abortion
- ◇ having given up children for adoption
- ◇ having prior marriages
- ◇ huge debt
- ◇ a homosexual lifestyle
- ◇ a past criminal record
- ◇ being pregnant

In rare cases, someone can be mistaken about the person he or she is marrying. Perhaps a woman thought she was marrying Tommy, but instead it was his scheming brother, Billy. Or, after months of Internet romance, a woman finally met and married Jim Smith, but that was only his screen name and he was someone else.

Error about marriage

Error about marriage is a misunderstanding about valid marriage that so strongly forms the will that the person isn't free to contract marriage as God intends. It used to be assumed that most people understood what marriage was. But that's just not true today.

This misunderstanding could easily exist, for example, for a young man who grew up in Mexico in an uneducated family that did not practice any religion, in a community where all the men had mistresses, the women knew it and seemed to accept it, and it was a longstanding social practice. No one taught him any different, so he did not really believe fidelity was necessary for marriage, nor did he intend to be faithful. Poor children in a family in the slums, who had no religious or moral training, lived with their grandmother, never saw their mother and had a different father each, might also have this misunderstanding. Exclusivity, permanence, and fidelity might be foreign concepts to them.

Simulation

Both parties have to really mean what they are saying at their wedding. The diamond of consent must be genuine—not a "simulated diamond." Imagine a woman who needs to marry someone in order to stay in the country, so a friend agrees to marry her to help out. Their exchange of "vows" is only a pretense.

Maybe someone has a deep animosity toward the Church and refuses to believe that marriage is a sacrament and internally wants no part of it, but is getting married in the Church to please the spouse or his or her parents.

Invalidity results when one or both of the parties did not truly intend to give a *free, full, faithful,* and *fruitful* consent.

⬦ The party(ies) could have excluded marriage *totally* (as in the case of the immigrant woman) or *partially* (some essential property or element, such as being open to children or intending to stay married forever).

⬦ One or both of them willfully intended not to give full consent.

⬦ Simulation must be a clear and positive act of the will, not just a general attitude.

Types of partial simulation include:

⬦ No intention of having children

⬦ No intention of staying completely faithful

⬦ No intention of staying married until death

⬦ No intention of doing all that it takes for the good of the spouse

⬦ No intention of entering into a sacrament or sacred bond

There has to be solid evidence and/or testimony to prove simulation. Even if the evidence is not strong enough, the resistance to the fullness of marriage might help in determining a "grave defect of discretion" or some mental, emotional, or psychological problem.

Condition

Conditional consent is no consent.

When someone puts a condition on the marriage, he or she turns the "I do" into "I do NOT." The condition can be about the past, present, or future. Examples include:

"If I ever find out you've had an abortion, it's over."

"I will only marry you if you keep that job/we move into that house."

"If you get sick and lose your job, it's over."

"If you can't support us in the way I am used to, I'll leave."

"If you ever have an affair, I'll divorce you."

Force and fear

Consent must be free of force or grave fear. If someone chose marriage because of an outside force or grave fear, the consent would be invalid.

Force is mostly physical. A true shotgun wedding can be an example.

The force or grave fear must be the cause of the marriage. Without it, no marriage would have taken place. "Everyone knew I hated Jose. But he threatened to kill my brother if I didn't marry him. I knew he would do it."

The fear must be grave. "What will people think?" may not be sufficiently grave unless it is part of other fears.

Grave fear can be physical, emotional, or a moral compulsion. Parents, pastors, and those in authority can instill fear, especially in the young, immature, and naïve. "My pastor said if I didn't marry my pregnant girlfriend, I would be committing mortal sin and if I died I'd go to Hell." "My parents said they would disown me and never speak to me again if I didn't marry him. I knew they would, because they did that to my pregnant sister and I haven't seen her for years."

The fear can be inflicted unintentionally by those in authority or power. Controlling or abusive parents and their immature adult children can fall into this pattern.

"Monica, honey, believe me, this is for your own good. You really don't have another choice."

"Don't worry. His drinking is not a problem. I've lived with your father's drinking for years, and you'll learn to handle it."

"The night before my wedding, I cried because I knew I was making a huge mistake, but my mother insisted it was just pre-wedding jitters and it would break her heart if I let her down. She's very sensitive and has heart problems. I just had to go through with it."

Peer pressure is usually not enough to be considered "grave fear," but it can be evidence along with other compulsions or fears of a Grave Defect of Discretion.

How you exchange vows (Expression of Consent)

In a valid exchange of consent, the bride and groom must be present to each other either in person or by a proxy (see next section). You can't get married over the phone or computer.

Those who marry must declare their consent in words, or if they can't speak, through appropriate and equivalent signs. That might even mean a nod of the head or a thumbs-up.

The vows must be exchanged in the physical presence of the Official Witness of the Church (the priest or deacon), either in person or by properly appointed proxy.

Proxies

A proxy is someone who has the authority to personally "stand in" for you by reason of a mandate naming him or her to do so, which you have issued. This is rare in the United States but more common in Europe. An example might be if one of the parties were unable to travel due to illness, job constraints, or military orders, and it was not possible for the parties to be together.

Interpreters

A valid marriage can be contracted through an interpreter.

However, the priest or deacon must be sure of the trustworthiness of the interpreter since *words matter*. Ask any contract lawyer. It's presumed that the person who needs the interpreter already has a full understanding of what is going on and what is required for valid consent.

Chapter 7

Form and Matter . . . Matter

I USED to enjoy speeding along Monterey Avenue at the posted limit of 65 mph where there were three lanes and open views of the Southern California desert. But one day I saw that the sign had been changed to 55 mph. *What? That's ridiculous,* I thought. I didn't see the necessity of the lower speed in this wide-open space, and I felt cheated. There hadn't been any major accidents here recently (that I knew of), and it just didn't make sense. I started to feel resentful that the state highway commission was trying to control me!

That's the attitude I also used to have toward rules and regulations I thought were "imposed" on Catholics by a bureaucratic Church . . . until I went through my own annulment and discovered the truth and wisdom behind it all. The way the Church requires people to get married—where, when, how, and by whom—has meaning, and it matters. We just don't understand, and yet like little children we don't want anyone telling us what to do!

I eventually did find out that four new side streets had been developed off Monterey Avenue, traffic count had increased dramatically, and there had been an increase in accidents. Hm-m-m. Maybe the state was trying to keep us all safer after all. Like the Church. The following is a brief summary of the technical form that the wedding ceremony must take to be valid.

Essential elements for valid form

The wedding must take place in the presence of the local ordinary (bishop) or pastor, or a priest or deacon delegated by either of them. Proper delegation is about respect and authority and ultimately is about protecting all parties. If your fiancé's priest-friend, who is going to perform the wedding ceremony, did not notify and get permission from your bishop or pastor, the whole wedding could be invalid—especially if he is not really a priest. (It happens!) The U.S. Bishops have secured permission to designate lay people to act as Official Ministers, but Alaska is the only state where this is used.

The exchange of vows must take place in the presence of two adult witnesses. Marriage is not just a personal choice of two people. It has both a private and a public dimension. Since every human person is part of the larger community, everything he or she does—both good and bad—has an effect on the whole community. Witnesses ensure the marriage is acknowledged, protected, and supported by the community.

In rare cases, a wedding may be valid where there are two witnesses but no Official Minister due to circumstances such as remote location where no priest or deacon was available for six months or more.

The Official Minister (properly delegated) must be the one to ask for and receive consent. He says, "Do you promise . . ." and he hears and receives the bride's and groom's individual "I do."

If a Catholic is marrying a non-Catholic (assuming permission or a dispensation has been granted), *in a ceremony that includes a non-Catholic clergy member, the Official Minister (Catholic) must secure consent from both parties.* Sometimes the wedding includes a Protestant minister, a Jewish rabbi, or another cleric but that minister is not to be the one who secures consent in a Catholic wedding. The Jewish bride can't say her vows to her rabbi and the Catholic groom to his priest and have a valid consent. There are some cases, however, in which the couple can be dispensed from having a Catholic minister, and then the properly delegated minister receives consent.

Who is bound by the proper form?

If either party is a baptized (or a professed) member of the Catholic Church who has not left the church by "a formal act" (such as joining another church) the wedding must follow canonical form. Simply put, anytime a Catholic marries "outside the church," it is an invalid marriage. In recent years, there has been a major flux of some poorly informed Catholics attending Protestant churches they feel are more "biblical" or where they "get better fed." Attendance by Catholics at a non-Catholic church may signal ignorance and certainly some dissatisfaction but may not be a formal act of defection. There are certain other factors that determine who is bound by form, and in rare cases, proper form can be dispensed with. Check with your local tribunal if this might apply to you.

Where you get married

Priests can't just officiate at a wedding anywhere they want—or where your pushy mother-in-law-to-be tells them to! The mandatory form of a valid marriage is (a) the properly delegated clergy and (b) two witnesses. The physical place will not invalidate an otherwise valid marriage, but it can make the ceremony illicit, or improper. The *who* is more important than the *where*.

In the late sixties and early seventies, there was an attempt to make liturgies less stuffy and more "user-friendly." But the pendulum swung the other way, and today the Church often suffers from an overly casual approach to the faith. A disturbing by-product of this swing is not just a lack of respect (and awe!) for the Real Presence of Christ in the Eucharist but only a reported 35 percent of Catholics even believe in it anymore. Getting married on a hilltop, at the beach, or in a hot air balloon—and writing your own vows—were move-ments away from what was thought to be unnecessar-ily stifling. But we've lost the mystery; the signs and symbols that mystically brought us into deeper realities that bring authentic life and love to marriage and all the sacraments.

To help restore and preserve the reality of Chris-tian marriage, a wedding involving at least one Catholic must be celebrated in:

⋄ a parish church
⋄ another church or oratory with the bishop's or pastor's permission
⋄ another suitable place with the permission of the bishop

What vows you say

Catholic wedding vows are intended to mystically and truly bring the couple into the mystery of the loving spousal union of Jesus the Bridegroom and His Bride, the Church. Jesus loves His Bride *freely, fully, faithfully,* and *fruitfully* and so the vows express a pledge of that kind of love:

"Do you come here of your own free will?" (*free*)

"Do you promise to be true to one another?" (*faithful*)

"In good times and in bad, in sickness and health, for richer or poorer, for better or worse, 'til death do you part?" (always and forever—*full*)

"Do you promise to receive the gift of children God will send?" (*fruitful*)

The couple may write their own vows, but any vows (from any source) that omit these essential properties (the four Fs of the "Diamond of Consent") may be invalid—not just because they are not prescribed by the Church but because *they do not reflect the vows that Jesus perpetually makes to His Bride.*

The ceremony

The Church has written the words and actions (rite) that best suit the sacramental reality of what happens at a Catholic wedding. Sometimes, by necessity, the rite may not be fully observed. But every ceremony—to be valid—must include appropriate *consent* that is given by the parties to the Official Minister on behalf of the Church.

Lack of form

When there is a lack of the proper Catholic form (as summarized above), the consent and therefore the marriage is invalid. This happens most often when a baptized Catholic makes no effort to comply with Church requirements, out of either willful defiance or simple ignorance. A civil ceremony is the usual example.

Defect of form

Even if a marriage appears valid, if it did not include one or more of the essential elements of form, it is invalid. This might happen because the priest or deacon failed to get delegation to officiate at the wedding. Or the parties did get married in their parish church, but they wrote their own vows that said they would remain together ". . . so long as we share the same path." In that case, there was no valid consent.

Formal and informal annulments

Informal case: When at least one party was Catholic and Catholic "form" was not followed.

Formal case: All other cases

When the invalid consent is due to *Lack of form* or *Defect of form* (at least one Catholic party not doing it the way prescribed by the Church), it is called an administrative or documentary case. Basic documents with names, dates, and places to support the petition are submitted to the tribunal for processing and recording. It takes a very short time compared with the "formal trial" of the issues in other cases. No formal trial of evidence is needed if these facts can be adequately proven by documents or physical evidence.

Pauline Privilege

A marriage between *two non-baptized persons* who have already civilly divorced can be dissolved "in favor" of the one who wants to convert to Christianity.

The converting party must not be the direct cause of the marital break-up.

The party who is not converting must have left the marriage following the civil divorce.

If the converting party wants to marry another, the non-baptized party must be asked about his/her willingness to receive baptism or at least leave in peace (not obstruct) the converting party.

If the non-converting party is truly unable to be contacted, refuses to participate, or abandons the converting spouse, it will not prevent the converting spouse from remarriage.

Petrine Dissolution (Privilege)

This is an administrative case that goes to Rome, where the Holy Father alone can grant this dissolution. At least one person remained unbaptized throughout the marriage, and now the couple is divorced.

The unbaptized person (petitioner) now either (a) wants to be baptized or (b) wants to marry a Catholic in the Church.

The petitioner was not the cause of the failed marriage.

There was no sexual intercourse after one (or both) was baptized.

The petitioner now intends to marry (a) a baptized person who is (b) free to marry and (c) was not involved in the breakup of the failed marriage.

If the petitioner gets baptized in a valid Christian baptism but does not convert to Catholicism, he or she must promise not to interfere with the new Catholic spouse's faith practice and to raise the children Catholic.

Non-consummation

After the couple exchanges vows, they are validly married.

That night in the honeymoon suite, they will strengthen their vows not just with words but with "body language" as they take their marriage to the highest level: consummation.

So, during the reception, as they glide around the dance floor, are they fully married? Yes. The exchange of vows (consent) *makes* the marriage. Consummation *strengthens* it. Consummation is also the final act that makes the marriage indissoluble.

But sometimes consummation doesn't occur for reasons that point to other problems in the relationship. When there is non-consummation, there is likely some other element that renders the consent invalid.

The Pope—for a just cause such as the psychological or spiritual well being of a person—may dissolve a marriage that has not been consummated. (Sexual activity before the wedding is not consummation). This is rare, but some examples might be marriage to a prisoner who has no conjugal rights, or marriages arranged for citizenship or to establish inheritance. Expert witnesses, usually psychologists, are often called in on this type of case.

Part 3

Preparing Your Petition

Chapter 8

Know What to Expect

IMAGINE the police have just arrested you for murder, thrown you into jail, and informed you that you would be on trial within the month. The first call you make? *Your attorney,* of course. In a similar way, when you realize you will need to prove your prior marriage was invalid, you'll first want to call your parish priest. In petitioning the Church tribunal for an annulment, you will participate in a process that is somewhat like a civil court, but *you're* not on trial; *the truth* is.

Get ready for "court"

In presenting your *Petition for a Declaration of Nullity,* you are claiming that your marriage was not valid.

Declaration of nullity

This is a declaration by the Church tribunal that what had the appearance of a marriage was in fact invalid according to canon law.

A "trial" will take place, but it is not about you or

your ex-spouse as much as it is about finding the truth. There's no blame. *Don't take this personally.* The truth is separate and apart from people, and the process is designed to seek truth while remaining compassionate toward the persons.

You are the Petitioner; your ex-spouse is the Respondent. Only a spouse can contest the validity of a marriage; no one else. You are asking the tribunal to confirm the truth of your marriage consent. The "trial" will take place either (first) in the diocese where the wedding took place, or (second) where the Respondent lives, or if certain requirements are met (third), where the Petitioner lives.

The tribunal has a panel of judges who will hear your case. They are skilled in canon law and may be trained clergy or laity. They regularly use trained professionals (such as assessors, auditors, doctors, psychologists, and psychiatrists) to assist them in getting to the truth.

Your marriage will be presumed valid unless proven otherwise. The burden of proof will be on the Petitioner to provide adequate evidence to support a claim of nullity.

You will be assigned an advocate to help you present your case. This person ideally should be a canon lawyer, but in reality those who can serve are few. At a minimum, your advocate should have had some type of formal training and a general understanding of both (a) sacramental marriage and (b) Church annulment. You begin the formal process when you submit your completed Petition, all required documents (such as a baptism certificate), and of course, a nominal processing fee to help cover clerical and office costs. No case is slowed or stopped by an inability to pay the fee.

The tribunal will assess whether the case has merit. If it does not have merit, the case is not accepted and a letter will suggest further consideration or analysis. If so, the ball starts rolling. The tribunal will also determine whether they have locational jurisdiction and will decide other pertinent technical issues.

The bishop will assign a "Defender of the Bond," who acts, in a certain sense, as the opposing counsel and will try to find authentic evidence that supports the validity of your marriage. He will try to prove your claim of invalidity wrong—if the truth supports it. His primary duty is to defend the indissolubility of marriage and the rights of the Respondent.

Your ex-spouse will be invited to participate. It's a fundamental right of the Respondent to know of and dispute (or affirm) the contentions and process. After all, it was his or her marriage, too. You will have to provide the current or last known contact information for your ex-spouse. If you don't know where he or she is, you will have to make a diligent search via currently available means, including using the Internet or even paying a private investigator. If it can be shown that you did everything reasonably possible to locate him or her, the case can proceed without your ex-spouse's knowledge. In some rare and special cases, where the petitioner may be in fear of his or her life, cause can be shown for no contact.

Your ex-spouse can throw the notice from the tribunal into the trash, and after no response, the case will proceed without him or her.

Your ex-spouse may decide to cooperate and send in truthful testimony that supports yours. In that instance, your ex-spouse can be a strong witness to the case, which will be extremely helpful.

Your ex-spouse may contest the petition and send in testimony that he or she believes supports the validity of the marriage. This may make the case more complicated.

The grounds will be set. Marriages are always assumed to be valid unless proved otherwise. If the tribunal determines there is merit to the case, it will determine which causes for nullity might apply. These causes for the failure of one or both of the parties to give valid consent are called "grounds."

Your witnesses will be contacted. It's a good idea to call your witnesses once you name them in your petition—or even beforehand—to let them know what to expect and that you or your advocate will be available to help answer any questions they may have. More about how to assist your witnesses is in chapter 13 of this book. *Ask that they act quickly!* Securing testimony from witnesses often causes the longest delay in a case.

The testimony will be collected and, under certain conditions, will be made available for review by parties. If experts such as psychologists are needed, they will be called in. Certain documents, such as copies of prenuptial agreements, may be requested. The parties and their advocates will have a short period—usually a few weeks—to review the testimony at the tribunal office. Don't worry; this information is confidential and not available to the public. If you have anything to add or refute, this is the time. If there is significant difficulty getting to the tribunal office, sometimes the testimony can be sent to the advocate and reviewed with him or her. No party is permitted to make copies or take notes, and everyone must sign an agreement not to sue any party, including the Church.

The testimony will be reviewed and a decision made. A panel of three tribunal judges determines formal cases, with a two-thirds vote based on moral certainty on the part of each judge. As in a civil court, this means the judge decides on evidence presented that establishes fact "beyond a reasonable doubt." They make their decision (the sentence) and state their reasoning in a letter sent to the parties and the advocate(s).

The decision will automatically go to a second court for review. The church has a well-planned system of checks and balances. Every decision is sent to another diocese's tribunal for review and evaluation by another set of judges before it is finalized.

Any appeal must be made within two weeks from the date of the decision. If you receive a negative decision, you may consider the appeal process. If two competent courts have studied the case, an appeal may be made with new testimony, or it may have to be made on new and different grounds with different testimony. These cases are rare. You must appeal by first writing to the judge of the first court. Under special circumstances, the appeal may go to Rome. For more information, talk to your advocate or call your local tribunal office.

If you receive a negative decision and do not appeal, you should definitely seek the counsel of a wise and holy priest, be it your pastor or another who understands the complexity of certain marriage issues. Don't worry; the Church has been around for a long time and is here to help you through *any* difficult times.

Myths and misconceptions

Warning! During the annulment process, you might not find the same warm, welcoming spirit you find with the men's group or the doughnut lady after morning Mass. Just like the seemingly cold civil-court clerk, judge, or bailiff, the people involved in the Church annulment process are focused on interpreting and upholding the law in their impartial search for truth. They're often trained to check their emotions at the door. This process requires a clear head and a keen mind to make sure the best efforts are made for you, your ex-spouse, and the sacrament of marriage. If you get good bedside manner, be thankful. If not, be thankful anyway.

Remember that an annulment:

◇ is not a Catholic divorce
◇ doesn't dissolve a marriage; it's a judicial finding that what appeared to be a valid marriage in fact was not
◇ can be grossly misunderstood by laity and clergy alike
◇ not deny the goodness of any love, affection, and shared life that existed between ex-spouses
◇ does not make children illegitimate (that is a civil word that arose as a means of protecting people's property and inheritance rights) because the church has always held that every child has great dignity, worth, and sanctity
◇ doesn't ex-communicate anyone

Start with your parish priest

Your parish priest has been given care of your soul and is available to help direct you through this process. Depending on your parish and the availability of other trained advocates, he may or may not serve as your advocate. If he does, I hope you will see that he is doing a competent job for you. But trust your instincts if things are confusing and do not seem to be going well. Just because he is a priest, he may not have the wisdom or the experience to be a good advocate; his gifts and talents may lie in other areas. So, stay open, educate yourself, and ask a lot of questions.

Read and research

Take an adult approach to being informed and involved in your case, even if it all seems foreign or overwhelming. Before you even begin the process, you can find out a lot about annulments and other church teachings from trusted Catholic sources such as www. Catholic.com. As St. Paul told the Thessalonians, "Test everything and hold on to what is good and shun every form of evil" (1 Thes 5:21-22). Read and research whatever areas interest you, and become an active participant in your annulment rather than a passive bystander. But let the tribunal do their work!

The Great Advocate

The annulment process can be confusing, intimidating, or overwhelming simply because it is so foreign to the average lay person. *But you are not alone.* By reason of your baptism and the lavish love of God our Father, you've already been given the greatest "advocate": The Holy Spirit.

On the night He was betrayed, Jesus told His disciples in the Upper Room, "I will pray the Father, and he will send you another Paraclete, to be with you forever" (Jn.14:16). The original Greek word, *Parakletos,* literally means "one who is called or appealed to" (from *parakalein,* "to call to one's assistance"). Like Jesus—who is the First Paraclete—the Holy Spirit is the Defender, the advocate who intercedes for us.

If you get anxious about the annulment process, remember the words of Jesus when He was sending His disciples off into the world:

"They will deliver you up to councils . . . you will be dragged before governors and kings. . . . When they deliver you up, do not be anxious how you are to speak or what you are to say . . . for it is not you who speak, but the Spirit of your Father speaking through you" (Mt 10:17-20; likewise Mk 13:11; Lk 12:12 says: "for the Holy Spirit will teach you in that hour what you ought to say").

Go to Him.

Implore His help.

He won't let you down.

Chapter 9

Get a Good Advocate

I RECALL one of the first cases Terri and I had working together.

A man seeking an annulment in a nearby parish had been sent to an elderly nun who would act as his advocate. The overworked pastor had assigned annulment cases to her, assuming perhaps that she would be proficient at anything because she was a religious. I know I am moving into sensitive territory here, but the local parish (and other organizations) may at times stuff available personnel into whatever position is open—regardless of the person's skill set. We need to make sure people are working within their strengths and not their weaknesses as much as possible.

Sister was a quiet, gentle soul who asked the standard questions, "How long were you married?" "Did you love each other when you got married?" "Why do you think the marriage failed?"

Not very probing, and each with the same standard answer: "Ten years. Yes, we were in love, and I'm not sure why the marriage failed. We just couldn't communicate very well and fell out of love."

These are not grounds for an annulment, but Sister wrote them down on the application form, had the man sign it, and sent it off to the tribunal. A year went by and Sister was transferred. The man called and wanted to know the status of his case.

Enter the ninjas

That's when Terri and I got called in. There *was* no case. The tribunal secretary asked us to help the man because there were no apparent grounds and there was nothing they could process. We agreed to take another look and called him in for an interview.

Poor guy. We definitely were not Sister. We dug, we probed, we pushed. I think I even leaned in toward him a little and said, "Are you sure there is not something else you are not telling us?" (I've used this successfully for years on the kids at home!) Okay, okay. I'm exaggerating a bit. But the point is that a good advocate has to establish trust with his or her "client" and then not be afraid to ask the hard questions. And with this man's open spirit and honest cooperation, we finally discovered more than one strong cause for granting nullity. He prepared his more-detailed questionnaire, and we submitted his case. Within the year he was granted a Decree of Nullity.

There have been many other times, though, when

we've put someone through the wringer with our questions and found no grounds whatsoever for a claim of nullity. In many cases, it becomes clear to us that two unhappy (and usually selfish) people just split up and now they want the blessing of the church to marry again. Or one of them wants desperately to remain married and the other simply left. Those are hard situations. When the bond appears to have been validly established and can't be proved otherwise, the marriage may not be broken, but hearts can be.

It's not always a matter of training or not. I think by our natural temperaments Terri and I had something Sister did not: an ability to ask hard, private questions that often cause embarrassment. Failed marriages are usually the result of something disordered that was there at the very beginning. It was our job to dig deeply and find out what that might be—like doctors who open up a patient and do NOT want to find cancer staring them in the face, but, to help the patient, they cut him open anyway.

"Did your parents *really* have a happy marriage?"

"Did either of you cheat on the other when you were dating?"

"Was there a history of sexual abuse in your or her childhood?"

"How often did you drink, and did you frequently pass out?"

"Was there any history of drug use?

Just as the medical team swabs on a topical antiseptic, Terri and I try to first assure the "patient" in our initial interview that going deep is necessary and it might hurt. I share about going through annulment and even a few shameful admissions of my own so they do not feel alone. We advise them that what they tell us remains strictly confidential (I changed a lot of the facts in this story, by the way). That we'll go slowly. That we love them.

And then we pass the Kleenex and begin.

What advocates do

The local pastor usually serves as or assigns an advocate, but either party in an annulment—the Petitioner or the Respondent—may freely appoint his or her own advocate, as long as the person is approved by the bishop. The advocate assists the client in:

- ◇ thoroughly interviewing the client carefully and with pastoral sensitivity
- ◇ determining the appropriate grounds for nullity
- ◇ preparing the petition and bringing out the decisive points
- ◇ obtaining the appropriate forms, documentation, and proofs
- ◇ selecting and assisting appropriate witnesses

What to look for in your advocate

Someone who is of legal age, trained, and has a good moral reputation

The advocate is approved by the bishop and usually must be Catholic, unless the bishop permits otherwise. A degree in canon law should be a requirement, but due to the shortage of persons who hold such a degree, many advocates serve under and in conjunction with those who have a degree. At the very least, an advocate should understand the technical requirements for presenting an annulment case.

Someone who will ask the hard questions

People accustomed to securing sensitive or potentially embarrassing information for their jobs can make excellent advocates or can serve as assistants to advocates. Like those in law enforcement, attorneys, or court personnel, those in the medical profession (doctors, nurses, and administrative staff) can also be good at getting to the heart of the matter. People who don't want to embarrass or offend someone should probably consider whether they are really suited or called to being an advocate.

Terri and I dig because we are seeking truth. If, based on the information a person has given us, we can find no reasonable evidence that the marriage consent was invalid, we tell the person we can't help him or her. Then we refer the person to the pastor for further counseling. Remember that the tribunal does not declare a marriage valid or invalid. Rather, it can declare only that there is—or is not—enough factual evidence to declare a marriage bond null.

Someone who will not judge our shame

A good advocate doesn't judge, just as a doctor doesn't exclaim, "Holy cow! I can't believe YOU have uterine cancer. You should be ashamed of yourself!" We are all broken; we are all wounded in some way or another. A good advocate remembers that.

Someone who understands reasons for invalidity

Terri and I have been trained at the diocesan level, and we both continue reading and attending workshops to sharpen our understanding. We need to know what constitutes grounds for an annulment so we can ask the right questions. We'll never be canon lawyers, but in our diocese we have a fabulous team of them with whom we work. They readily take our calls, read and answer our emails, and help us in our job. Some priests, deacons, religious, and lay persons are highly educated and beautifully skilled at this job; others are not.

Someone who speaks your language or is sensitive to language barriers

We make marriage vows with words of love. We divorce and petition for nullity with legal words. We tell our story in our own words. Words matter. If there might be some language problems that would make you or your witnesses' testimony difficult to read or understand, unclear, or insufficient, ask for help.

Someone who will read, review, and help you in the narrative petition

It's difficult for many people to tell their story adequately, much less to stay focused on the particular grounds they are trying to support. A good advocate will read and review the first draft of the Petition and make appropriate suggestions that would assist the tribunal in understanding the fullness of truth. *We assist—never instruct—the Petitioner or the witnesses.*

Terri and I have put our diocese's petition in a Microsoft Word document so the client can go home, make a copy, and start typing out his or her story. We email back and forth with questions and answers until the Petition narrative is clear and strong. For those who do not use a computer, we suggest they get a close and trusted friend or family member—who can respect privacy—to help.

It's not a good idea to have the advocate write the Petitioner's responses.

But there can be cases where the petitioner simply cannot compose the information into a logical narrative. Sometimes I have had people come into my office, sit on the couch next to my desk, and tell their story while I type. I keep a box of Kleenex there, too.

When you have to present a case, you need someone who:

- ◇ understands the law
- ◇ knows how the legal system works and is comfortable in it
- ◇ has a strong support staff
- ◇ has strong moral character
- ◇ will defend, not you as a person, but the truth of your case

Once you have chosen or accepted this person to be your advocate (defender), you expect him or her to:

- ◇ listen carefully to your full story
- ◇ ask probing questions to get to the deeper truths
- ◇ be aware of and sensitive to cultural attitudes and conditions
- ◇ investigate the other side
- ◇ anticipate the Respondent's claims
- ◇ challenge you to tell the whole truth
- ◇ prepare your case in light of the law
- ◇ help you tell your story in the way that proves your case

Chapter 10

Start at the Beginning

CHERYL kicked off her high heels and walked toward the bathroom of the hotel honeymoon suite carrying her little red travel valise. Her new husband kissed her lightly on the back of the neck as she went by.

"What's in *there*, darling?" he asked, not really caring at all. Cheryl smiled sweetly.

"Oh, just a little something I brought just for you!"

He knew she'd pull out something sheer and delicate, and he delighted in the thought.

But what if he could really *see what was in the bag?*

When we get married, each person brings "baggage" from the past that we hope is just a small overnight case. Instead, the passing of time may reveal their huge steamer trunk like the ones clowns use at the circus: a bottomless pit of problems. If those problems from the past (fears, pressures, addictions, gross immaturity or selfishness, personality disorders, abuse issues, and more) are sufficiently "grave," they can adversely affect the ability of the couple to give valid consent. Those problems usually start in childhood and get packed into that little valise we bring to the church.

This is not a witch hunt

Before you begin the process, please remember that everyone has problems and even the best marriages have conflict. Everyone will struggle with fears and selfishness until the day he or she dies. The graces that come through a valid sacramental marriage can help lift people up to a higher degree of loving each other rightly. Grace helps us all overcome all kinds of sin and selfishness. Divorce does not do this.

That said, some people are emotionally crippled—often through no fault of their own—or have gravely disordered ways of thinking about life and love. They can try with all their might to have a good marriage but *from the beginning* there was something in the way of their being able to give valid consent.

Cultural attitudes and influences can play a significant part in what a bride or groom thinks, believes, or understands about the essential rights and obligations of marriage. A pattern Terri and I have seen is an absolute loyalty by a bride to her mother or father over her spouse in some cultures; or a commonly practiced and firm belief that you can love a wife and still keep a mistress.

Problems that happen well into the marriage may or may not support an annulment. *The focus needs to be on the time of consent,* not necessarily ten years into the marriage. However, if the patterns or events seen later in the relationship can be reasonably and logically tied to the day of the wedding, they might help support a case.

Mary was still sleeping with her former boyfriend at the time she married Jeff. She went back and forth to the boyfriend the entire marriage. Those later affairs point to what was present at the time she said, "I do." Tom slept with his secretary after twelve years of marriage, but he'd been faithful during courtship and truly did love his wife. He just grabbed a quick, easy fix for the frustration he was feeling in his marriage. His later affair does not negate what was present at the time of consent. Affairs are usually symptoms, not root causes.

The following questions are not intended to drum up support for an annulment, but to uncover hidden truths from which the original marital consent can be declared null. As you answer the questions, remember:

◇ Mark the ones you want to discuss with your advocate.
◇ Yes and no answers are too short for this type of questionnaire. Please give as much explanation as is relevant and ask your advocate if you need to expand your answers or be briefer.
◇ Answer as many questions as you can. You

don't have to answer each one, but let them help you think back and identify what was in your "suitcase" on the wedding day.

◇ Avoid general answers such as, "My ex-spouse was an alcoholic." Instead, give some specifics such as, "My ex-spouse drank every night after work and would pass out in front of the TV. On weekends the drinking would start in the afternoon, and sometimes he or she would get sick and stay in bed on Sunday with a hangover. This went on while we were dating and lasted into the marriage."

Your baptismal status

◇ Were you both baptized Catholics?
◇ Did one of you convert and the other leave?

Your parents' marriage

The annulment petition begins by asking about your parents' marriage and the marriage of the parents of your ex-spouse. Why? That's where you both first learned about how to be a husband or wife. It was your first view of marriage, and who knows what beliefs about marriage you brought to the altar?

◇ Was one of your parents overly dominant and the other extremely passive?

What negative patterns did you see from
this?

◇ Were there any terrible fights you remember? If so, how frequent were they? Give an
example.

◇ Was there drinking, drugs, gambling, or
other addiction that affected their marriage
and the family life? Give an example.

◇ Were your parents faithful to each other? If
not, explain.

◇ Were either of your parents depressed?

◇ Were they able to show loving affection to
each other? Explain.

◇ Did your parents divorce? How old were
you at the time? Tell the story.

◇ Did you have stepparents? How was the
subsequent marriage?

◇ Did your parents avoid problems and never
talk about things?

◇ What were the husband and wife roles you
thought were normal in a marriage? (Example: wife should be financially supported
and not have to work; husband should be
able to stay out all night and not get flack.)

◇ What husband- and wife role-expectations
did you have of your spouse that were not
met in the marriage?

Your ex-spouse's parents' marriage

Explain to the best of your knowledge what kind of marriage your ex-spouse's parents had and how it may have affected his or her ability to enter marriage.

◇ Was one of his or her parents overly dominant and the other extremely passive? Was that pattern brought into your relationship? Explain.

◇ Were there any terrible fights? If so, how frequent were they? Give an example.

◇ Was there drinking, drugs, gambling, or other addiction that affected their marriage and the family life? Give an example.

◇ Were his or her parents faithful to each other? If not, explain.

◇ Were either of his or her parents depressed?

◇ Were they able to show loving affection to each other? Explain.

◇ Did his or her parents divorce? How old was your ex-spouse at the time? Tell the story.

◇ Did he or she have stepparents? How was the subsequent marriage?

◇ Did his or her parents avoid problems and never talk about things?

◇ What were the husband and wife roles he or she thought were normal in a marriage? (Example: wife should be financially supported and not have to work; husband should be able to stay out all night and not get flack)

◊ What husband-and-wife role-expectations did your ex-spouse have of you that were not met in the marriage?

Your childhood home

These questions are not intended to be a two-hundred-page autobiography but should help point to the cause of any problems in your courtship or marriage. The following list is also not meant to be exhaustive, so if you think of anything else that might be relevant, include it.

◊ What was your relationship with your mother like? Explain any difficulties.

◊ What was your relationship with your father like? Explain any difficulties.

◊ Did anyone other than your biological parents raise you? Why? Explain any difficulties.

◊ What was your relationship with your siblings like? Explain any difficulties.

◊ Where did you fit in your family (oldest child, middle child, youngest child), and were there any problems?

◊ Was discipline healthy or abusive? Explain.

◇ Was there any unusual behavior by anyone in your family? How did your parents and the rest of your family deal with it? Give examples.

◇ Did you feel loved and encouraged as a child?

◇ What role did religion and faith play in your family?

◇ Was your childhood home happy or not? Explain any difficulties.

◇ As a child, were you ever abused physically, verbally, emotionally, or sexually by anyone in or outside your family? Please be honest and give examples. How did this affect you?

◇ Were there any legal or criminal problems in your family? Explain.

◇ Was anyone in your family ever institutionalized, hospitalized, or otherwise treated for a significant emotional or psychological problem?

◇ Did anyone in your family get pregnant out of wedlock? How was that handled?

◇ Were you anxious to get out of the house? If so, why?

◇ Were you afraid to leave home? If so, why?

◇ Do you think you were spoiled, pampered, or immature? Explain.

◇ How old were you when you first moved out?

Your ex-spouse's childhood home

These questions should help point to the cause of any problems in your courtship or marriage. This list is also not meant to be exhaustive, so if you think of anything that might be relevant, include it.

◇ What was your ex-spouse's relationship with his or her mother like? Explain any difficulties.

◇ What was your ex-spouse's relationship with his or her father like? Explain any difficulties.

◇ Did anyone other than your ex-spouse's biological parents raise him or her? Why? Explain any difficulties.

◇ What was your ex-spouse's relationship with siblings like? Explain any difficulties.

◇ Where did your ex-spouse fit into the family, and were there any problems?

◇ Was discipline healthy or abusive? Explain.

◇ Was there any unusual behavior by anyone in the family? How did your ex-spouse's parents and the rest of the family deal with it? Give example.

◇ Did your ex-spouse feel loved and encouraged as a child?

◇ What role did religion and faith play in the family?

◇ Was your ex-spouse's childhood home happy or not? Explain the difficulties.

◇ As a child, was your ex-spouse ever abused physically, verbally, emotionally, or sexually by anyone in or outside the family? Please be honest and give examples. How did this affect your ex-spouse?

◇ Were there any legal or criminal problems in the family? Explain.

◇ Was anyone in the family ever institutionalized, hospitalized, or otherwise treated for a significant emotional or psychological problem?

◇ Did anyone in the family get pregnant out of wedlock? How was that handled?

◇ Was your ex-spouse anxious to get out of the house? If so, why?

◇ Was your ex-spouse afraid to leave home? If so, why?

◇ Do you think your ex-spouse was spoiled, pampered, or immature? Explain.

◇ How old was your ex-spouse when he or she first moved out?

Childhood abuse

Survivors of child abuse are often high-functioning and abuse problems may not be easily detectable by casual observation. This is a place to talk more about specific abuse and how it may have affected you or your ex-spouse's ability to give valid consent. Include rape, incest, long periods of physical or emotional neglect, drugs, abandonment, frequent moving around, or an inability to attach.

- ◇ Did you or your ex-spouse ever receive therapy or counseling for childhood problems? Explain.
- ◇ Did you or your ex-spouse struggle with abusing your own or other people's children? Explain.

Criminal activity

- ◇ Was either of you involved in any type of criminal activity?
- ◇ When, how old were you or your ex-spouse, and how often/long did it occur?
- ◇ Were you or your ex-spouse ever prosecuted or jailed?
- ◇ How did this affect your courtship or marriage?

Homosexual attraction

The Church considers this a particular and sensitive area for many men and women. Struggles often start in childhood and sometimes make it impossible for someone to marry—even when they desire marriage. If you haven't already addressed this in a previous section, please include information here.

◇ Have you or your ex-spouse ever struggled with same-sex attraction (SSA)? If so, how did this affect your courtship and marriage? Please explain and give sufficient examples.

◇ Were you sexually initiated by a person of the same sex?

◇ Have you or your ex-spouse ever been involved in a same-sex relationship or life-style prior to, during, or after the marriage? Please explain.

◇ Have either of you received counseling for this?

◇ Do you or your ex-spouse still struggle with this?

History of addictions

Addictions can be severe or mild, and they indicate, at least temporarily, a person's inability to make good decisions. Prior to and at the time of the wedding, did any of the items in the list below apply to you or your ex-spouse? Give specific example for each and indicate (1) when it started, (2) its frequency, (3) how it affects your home, your work, and your relationships, and (4) whether treatment—such as twelve-step programs—has been sought or received.

◇ Chain-smoking
◇ Compulsive overeating
◇ Alcohol use
◇ Marijuana use
◇ Prescription drug abuse
◇ Use of illegal drugs and narcotics
◇ Gambling
◇ Pornography
◇ Sex addiction
◇ Compulsive shopping/buying

Chapter 11

Tell about the Courtship and Wedding

WHAT happened during the time you dated and decided to marry is extremely important in showing what state of mind you both were in at the time you said, "I do."

A common problem among couples who begin sexual activity before marriage, is that such activity *blinds them* and *binds them* to each other. Sex is very powerful—as God intended—but it sweeps us away before we know a person and establish a mature relationship. Questions about sexual intimacy are not meant to be intrusive, but to see whether it clouded *good judgment* that should have been present at the time of consent.

In some cultures, it's a given that you will marry the person with whom you first have sex. This has caused many couples to feel duty-bound to attempt marriage before they were truly ready or able.

Your personality type

Extreme personality behaviors are sometimes helpful in assessing (with other factors) the maturity or ability of the people to give valid consent.

◇ Was either of you the extremely shy, intro-
verted type?

◇ Was one of you an extreme, outgoing "party
animal" type?

◇ Was either of you prone to isolation or
depression?

◇ Was either of you an extreme perfectionist?

◇ Was either of you often disengaged or
apathetic?

◇ Did one of you value keeping peace so
much that you would go along with things
you did not like?

Your prior dating experience

◇ How long had you been dating other people
before your ex-spouse?

◇ How many other serious relationships had
you had?

◇ Did you have any live-in relationships?
How many, with whom, and what
happened?

◇ Was there a common pattern of your
past relationships (short-lived, long-term,
eager to marry, fear of commitment, abusive, etc.)?

◇ Had you been married before? If so,
describe the marriage.

Your dating relationship with your ex-spouse

- ◇ Were you blood relatives?
- ◇ Were you both baptized Christians?
- ◇ How old were you both when you first met, and started dating?
- ◇ How mature do you think each of you was? (Chronological age does not necessarily mean someone is mature or immature.)
- ◇ What did you think of each other at first?
- ◇ What common interests did you have?
- ◇ How much time did you normally spend together in a week?
- ◇ How soon did you have any sexual intimacy?
- ◇ How soon did you have sexual intercourse?
- ◇ Was someone pushy or forceful?
- ◇ After engaging in sexual activity, did you start thinking this was the person you should or would marry?
- ◇ When and how did the topic of marriage come up?
- ◇ What were your initial feelings about it, and why?
- ◇ How long did you date before the wedding?
- ◇ Were there any breakups during the dating/ courtship period? Explain why and what happened.

⋄ How did you and your ex-spouse handle arguments?

⋄ What did you mostly argue about?

The proposal

The decision to marry is serious and should be carefully talked about and planned. Being sure, ready, and excited usually results in a formal proposal. Sometimes when "the subject just comes up," it may indicate fear, insecurity, or reluctance on at least one side, or someone waiting for the other one to make the move. Some just allow themselves to be led by the other. These can indicate gross immaturity.

⋄ When did the subject of marriage come up?

⋄ Who brought it up, and why?

⋄ Was there any pressure from parents or friends?

⋄ How did you feel, and why? How did your ex-spouse feel?

⋄ How much had you talked about marriage?

⋄ Were there any fears on either side? What were they?

⋄ Were you or your ex-spouse afraid that no one else might marry you?

⋄ Were you forced in any way to marry this person or did you force him or her?

⋄ Were you or your ex pregnant or thinking you/she might be?

◇ Had you already had any children together?
◇ Was there a formal proposal? Tell what happened.
◇ Was there a ring? If not, why?
◇ Was there any reluctance to accept?
◇ After the proposal, were there any doubts on either side? Explain.
◇ If you had children from a prior marriage, did you tell them? Why or why not?
◇ Was there a formal engagement party? Why or why not?
◇ Were your friends and family happy about the engagement or not? Explain.

The courtship

◇ How long were you engaged before the wedding?
◇ Did you discuss having children?
◇ Did you talk about important issues, such as in-laws, family, money, and the roles each of you would assume in the marriage?
◇ Did things change after the proposal? If so, explain.
◇ Were there any big arguments during courtship (the engagement period)? Explain.
◇ Was there any infidelity during this time? Explain.
◇ Did either of you keep delaying the wedding for any reason? Explain.

Marriage preparation

Premarital counseling and education is not mandatory for validity, but its absence may help support the presumption that one or both of the parties did not fully understand the seriousness of the "essential rights and obligations" of marriage.

- ◇ Did you have any formal wedding preparation in your diocese? Describe the length in days, type of program, and topics covered.
- ◇ Did you have any informal marriage preparation from your pastor or others?
- ◇ Did your pastor or anyone else in the church advise that one or both of you was "not ready" for marriage? Explain.
- ◇ If you and your ex-spouse were Catholic, were you both practicing your faith? Explain.
- ◇ If you were Catholic, had you received the Sacrament of Confirmation before the wedding? If not, why not?
- ◇ Had you both been advised to go to Confession and receive the Holy Eucharist before the wedding? (The presence of serious sin does not impact validity.)
- ◇ Were either of you not practicing or had you rejected Christianity or Catholicism in general?

⋄ Did either of you agree to get married "in the Church" to appease the other or because of pressure from friends or family members?

⋄ Did you both understand and agree that marriage was for life, no matter what? If not, explain.

⋄ Did you both understand and agree that marriage required emotional, physical, and sexual faithfulness at all times?

⋄ Did you both understand and agree that marriage was not about "his money" and "her money"?

⋄ Did you both understand and agree that you were to remain open to children?

⋄ Did either of you tell the other that a pregnancy should be aborted?

⋄ Were the Church teachings on sex, marriage, and birth control explained clearly and adequately to you before marriage?

⋄ Was either of you not open to children? Did one of you hope to change the other's mind after marriage?

Prenuptial agreements

⋄ Was there a prenuptial agreement? Please describe and attach a copy to the petition.

⋄ Whose idea was the prenup?

⋄ What was the reasoning behind it?

- ◇ Did you both agree, or was there some argument?
- ◇ Did you discuss it with anyone before or after the wedding?
- ◇ Did your friends and family know about it?

Conditions

- ◇ Did you put any conditions (sexual, financial, physical, social, religious, medical, legal, etc.) on the relationship or marriage?
- ◇ Did your ex-spouse put any conditions on the relationship or marriage?

Force or fear

- ◇ Was either of you afraid that if you did not marry, something bad would happen? Explain.
- ◇ Was either of you afraid of staying in a current living condition or family condition and saw marriage as an escape? Explain.
- ◇ Did you feel equal in the relationship? If not, explain.

Secrets

- ◇ Were there any secrets that were withheld from the other prior to marriage out of fear the other would not go through with the wedding? What were they? Explain.

(Typical secrets might include: *sterility;
permanent impotence; childhood sexual abuse
and trauma; prior or ongoing affairs; past
abortions; legal troubles; sexually transmit-
ted diseases; homosexual tendencies; sexual
fetishes; trickery or fraud; apostasy* (rejecting
the faith); *addictions, including pornography;
large amounts of debt; prior marriages; children given up for adoption; etc.*)

The wedding plans

◇ Where and how did you get married?
◇ Who decided the date and location?
◇ Who paid for the wedding?
◇ Who decided who would be on the invita-
   tion list?
◇ Did one of you kick the other's friends or
   family off the list? Explain.
◇ Was one of you in charge and the other one
   just going along to keep peace?
◇ Who made most of the decisions about the
   wedding plans?
◇ Was there any pressure from the parents or
   the pastor?
◇ Did either of you get "cold feet" as the day
   drew near? Explain.
◇ Did anyone know about these hesitations or
   fears?

- ◇ Were there any arguments over wedding details? Explain.
- ◇ Did any family member or close friend strongly object to the marriage? Explain.
- ◇ Did any family member or close friend refuse to come to the wedding because of the person or circumstances under which you were marrying?

Bachelor / bachelorette parties

- ◇ Was there any excessive drinking, drug use, or inappropriate sexual behavior at these events? Explain.
- ◇ Were there any secrets or arguments that ensued before or after the parties?
- ◇ Did any of your close friends advise you not to marry this person? Explain.
- ◇ Did you want to call the wedding off but were afraid of what a parent or others might say or do? Explain.
- ◇ Did you share this information with anyone (potential witness)?

The big day

- ◇ What were your thoughts and feelings on your wedding day?
- ◇ How did your ex-spouse feel?

◇ Were there any last-minute warnings not to get married from family or friends? Explain.

◇ Was either of you significantly late for the ceremony? If so, explain.

◇ Was either of you substantially hung over from the night before?

◇ Did either of you drink the day of the wedding or before the ceremony? How much? Why?

◇ Was either of you intoxicated when you said, "I do"? Did anyone know it (potential witness)?

◇ Did you get into any arguments the night before or the day of the wedding? Explain.

◇ Were there any major disappointments?

◇ Do you feel the day was inappropriately "all about the bride"?

◇ Was one of you more *the center of attention* with friends and family than the other? Explain.

The presider

◇ Did you get married in a Catholic church?

◇ Was the Official Minister a Catholic priest or deacon? If not, explain.

◇ If the priest was a friend from outside the parish, do you know whether he

contacted the parish office and was properly delegated?
◇ Did the priest or deacon ask both of you (for consent) to recite your wedding vows to each other?

The witnesses

◇ Did you have two adult witnesses to your exchange of vows?

The vows

◇ Did you recite vows given to you by the parish wedding coordinator or priest?
◇ Do you remember what they were?
◇ Do you have any video of the wedding ceremony?
◇ Did you write your own vows that replaced the Catholic vows? (Sometimes a pastor will permit the couple to recite words of love to each other separate and apart from the official vows, either after the wedding or outside the marriage rite. These do not replace the Catholic vows.)

The reception

- ◇ Did you have a wedding reception?
- ◇ Was it fun and pleasant?
- ◇ Was there any inappropriate behavior or arguments that ensued? Explain.
- ◇ Did your ex-spouse embarrass you in any way?

The honeymoon

- ◇ Was the marriage (ever) consummated? If not, explain.
- ◇ How was the wedding night?
- ◇ Were there any problems with sex? Explain.
- ◇ Was the rest of the trip enjoyable for you both?
- ◇ Were there any arguments that ensued?
- ◇ Did you or your ex-spouse have any early regrets?

Chapter 12

Tell about the Marriage and Divorce

The first year

- ◇ When did you first realize the marriage was not right?
- ◇ Were there any immediate problems in your relationship? Explain.
- ◇ Did either of you suddenly "change your mind" about children and/or seek sterilization?
- ◇ Did either of you spend too much money that caused arguments?
- ◇ Were you still living with parents or in-laws? Why?
- ◇ Did you attend church together regularly? If not, explain.
- ◇ Did either of you suffer from depression?

Your character

- ◇ What was your priority in life when you married?

- ◇ How did that affect your marriage?
- ◇ What problems did you struggle with in courtship and the early part of marriage?
- ◇ Were you always honest?
- ◇ Could you communicate openly and clearly about anything with your ex-spouse? Explain.
- ◇ What were your biggest fears during the marriage?
- ◇ When you fought, who or what did you turn to in order to feel better?
- ◇ How often did you talk to your mother or father during a typical week?
- ◇ Were you still too emotionally connected with a parent? (Was he or she your "best friend"?)
- ◇ Do you think your ex-spouse put the children (or someone else) before you in your marriage? Explain.
- ◇ Did you cause significant problems by making bad judgments?

Character of your former spouse

- ◇ What was his or her priority in life when you married?
- ◇ How did that affect your marriage?

◇ What problems did he or she struggle with in courtship and the early part of your marriage?

◇ Was he or she always honest?

◇ Could he or she communicate openly and clearly about anything with you? Explain.

◇ What were his or her biggest fears during the marriage?

◇ When you fought, who or what did he or she turn to in order to feel better?

◇ How often did your ex-spouse talk to his or her mother or father during a typical week?

◇ Was he or she still too emotionally connected with a parent? (Was the parent your ex-spouse's "best friend"?)

◇ Did your ex-spouse think you put the children first over the marriage?

◇ Did your ex-spouse cause significant problems by making bad judgments?

Your first big fight

◇ What was your first big fight about?

◇ What were the majority of your arguments about?

◇ How did you resolve problems?

◇ Did either of you suffer from physical, emotional, or sexual abuse in the marriage? Explain, and describe how often.

Parenting problems

⋄ Was either of you overly attached to the children? Explain.

⋄ Was either of you unable to bond with the children? Explain.

⋄ Was there physical, emotional, or sexual incest? Explain.

⋄ Were there any unusual discipline problems?

Breaking up

⋄ Did you break up and get back together during the marriage?

⋄ When? How many times? Explain the situation.

Separation

⋄ When did you first separate and why?

⋄ Who left and how long was the separation?

⋄ Did you get back together?

⋄ When was the final separation?

Divorce

⋄ Who filed for divorce?

⋄ How did you feel about it?

⋄ When was the divorce filed?

◇ When was it final?
◇ Was the divorce "amicable"?
◇ If the divorce took a long time, explain why.
◇ Were there long, drawn-out battles over money, property, or child support?
◇ Were there battles over custody and visitation?

Prior marriages

◇ Had you or your ex-spouse been married before this marriage? Here you can list any/all prior marriages separately (including names, dates, and locations) with documentation that includes:
  - *Civil marriage certificate* (signed, with recording date)
  - *Church marriage/convalidation certificate* (with date, location, and name of Official Minister)
  - *Civil divorce decree* (signed, with recording date)
  - *Church Decree of Nullity* (if applicable)
◇ Had either of you been a priest or religious who had taken a perpetual vow of chastity? Here you should provide a Rescript of Dispensation.

Convalidations

When two people who are already civilly married are able to marry within the Catholic Church, they can have their marriage "convalidated." The common phrase is "having your marriage blessed" but convalidation is far more than a blessing: *it elevates the civil contract to a sacrament—an unbreakable covenant.* Sacraments are unique, mystical encounters with Christ—the married couple gets "caught up" into the mystical marriage of Jesus and His Bride, and they can draw upon all the graces that flow from that holy union.

The Church says that the marriage *sacrament* started the day of convalidation. So, in an annulment case, the time of "consent" in this instance would be the day they had the marriage convalidated, not the day of the civil ceremony.

If you had this marriage convalidated, you'll need to provide the date, location, and a copy of the Church certificate.

Remarriage(s)

⋄ Has either of you remarried since this marriage?

⋄ If not, do you plan to remarry? Is the person you intend to marry free to marry within the church?

Chapter 13

Choose Good Witnesses

Your ex-spouse

IF YOU can get the understanding and cooperation of your ex-spouse, do so. Your ex-spouse may be your best witness if his or her testimony supports the facts in your Petition.

Yes, she drank a lot even when we were dating.

Yes, I have always been gay and now I am happy I'm "out."

Yes, I loved her, but I did hide my gambling debt from the beginning.

You can suggest that your ex-spouse get a separate advocate. Your advocate can help get you names and contact information.

Selecting good witnesses

The issues focus on *the time of consent*: the wedding day. Good witnesses are those who knew you before and right after the wedding and who could speak to what they knew, saw, or heard as to fears, pressures, problems, your state of mind, and your abilities when you said, "I do."

Who knew you and/or your former spouse best?

Who knew the situation best?

◇ Wedding attendants
◇ Best friends
◇ Family members
◇ The priest who officiated
◇ Marriage prep instructor(s)
◇ Your therapist
◇ Your doctor
◇ Mutual friends
◇ Your parish priest
◇ Employers or coworkers

Assisting the witnesses

In a civil court, it's a violation to "instruct" your witness, implying that you have told him or her what to say, regardless of the truth. Every witness needs to be free to tell what they saw, heard, or know without *anyone* leading them. That protects everyone.

Neither you nor your advocate is to get overly involved in their response. But to call a witness into court without any general assistance is sure to result in not only ineffective but damaging testimony. Your witnesses *will* need some help. Here's an example.

Jim's cousin, Sue, knew that his ex-spouse was a heavy drinker and probably needed to go into AA when she was a teenager. Sue agreed to witness to the drinking but was afraid to be specific and defame anyone's character. So she wrote, "Mary liked to drink a lot. Jim did not like that." Jim's advocate helped Jim explain to Sue that she needed to give more detail, assuring her it was about the truth, not about the persons. So Sue amended her questionnaire to read, "Mary was a lovely girl in many regards, but she drank to the point of passing out most of the time I was at their home. Once she even threw up all over the living room floor, and my husband and I left early." Her testimony was much more effective after being "coached," not instructed.

When the witnesses are reluctant to tell the whole truth

I had a recent conversation with a witness in a case where he was struggling with completing the questionnaire sent to him. I offered to listen to his oral testimony and assist him in putting it to paper. The grounds in the case were, in part, the grave lack of due discretion where both the bride and groom were extremely emotionally immature and not ready to make a lifelong commitment. It's often difficult to gather enough testimony to sufficiently prove gross immaturity and usually takes a lot of specific examples of the history, attitudes, and behaviors of the couple.

"The petitioner says you were his best man at the wedding and were at the bachelor party a few nights before. Can you tell me about that?"

"Well, whoa! *[Laughter.]* The bachelor party was a night of debauchery, alright. . . . We did lots of alcohol, drugs, and there was a stripper. We were definitely party animals who didn't want to grow up. Ha ha ha."

Oh brother, I thought.

"What kind of drugs?" I asked him.

"You name it. Pot, cocaine. *Lots* of coke."

"And the stripper? Was there anything that went on between her and the groom?"

"Oh, yeah! Her and everybody."

I winced.

"And you were there on the day of the wedding where everyone started drinking that morning. Can you tell me about that?"

"Well, the bride and groom were both *really* hung over, but everyone started drinking again the next morning. The girls and the guys. Hair of the dog, ya know! *[More laughter.]* I don't remember the church part, but I sure do remember the party!"

"How much did the groom drink? Do you recall?"

"Oh, yeah! We laughed about it for years. He slammed down enough tequila to kill a mule just before the ceremony. And she was so drunk she passed out on the reception dance floor!"

I had a pit in my stomach just listening. I knew the

divorced parties and the pain they had suffered. They were both decent people who'd had beautiful children, but clearly they had not been ready for marriage the way God intended.

"So, in your opinion, do you think he was really ready to settle down?"

"Oh [bleep] no! He'd been putting off marriage for decades and usually just lived with his girlfriends. But they were getting older, and she was pushing the whole thing."

"Okay, good. Please put all that in your testimony since it speaks very well to [the Petitioner's] immaturity, okay?"

"What? *I can't put that down!*"

"What do you mean?"

"I can't say strippers and cocaine and all that."

"You *have to* if you're going to tell the truth. Believe me, these guys at the tribunal have heard it all. Just like priests. They're in the business of helping hurting people get to the truth. They won't think badly of anyone or make judgments."

The witness listened as I encouraged him to be as honest and specific as possible, and he said he would think it over. A few days later, he sent an email copy of what he sent to the tribunal:

[The Petitioner] liked to party and was not really ready for marriage in my opinion.

That was it.

He was an excellent witness but his testimony was ineffective because he was afraid to say anything too "bad" about anyone. He also had a juvenile perception of "the Church" and—almost like a good little Catholic school boy—he'd told me that he wanted his testimony to be "respectful." Arghhh! I was so frustrated. I told the petitioner that he had to get some more witnesses and to not try to force any more out of this friend.

So in assisting the witnesses, please remember the following:

They may not want to say anything bad about others. They may still be friends with your ex-spouse, or even if they aren't, they may feel as if they are betraying someone by telling "secrets." Gossip is still a sin, and some don't know how to differentiate between helpful testimony and tongue-wagging. One witnesses shared that she felt like a "little Russian child turning her parents in to the secret police." You'll need to respect that; keep encouraging them but don't press if they keep resisting.

They may feel overwhelmed by all the questions. If you let the tribunal know that a witness needs a little extra time, they will usually hold the case open. Offer to have your advocate talk with them. Sometimes if they have a specific and pointed story that will provide strong evidence—such as being present the night the bride screamed at the groom that she was marrying him only because she was pregnant—they might just focus on that and skip the other questions.

They may not know how to focus on the grounds. Your case for nullity will focus on specific reasons—the grounds. The witness may write pages and pages about your family, your dating, your marriage, and maybe mention the affair ten years down the road, but never talk about the prenuptial agreement or the fact that everyone knew the bride was cheating on the groom, even at the time of the wedding. Explain the grounds as best you can, and ask them to focus on them.

They may not know how to tie marital problems to the beginning. Nullity must focus on the time of the wedding. Problems that occurred later in the relationship are important only to the degree they speak to what lies, secrets, infidelities, selfishness, immaturity, addictions, or other factors were present when the couple said, "I do." In one case, the bride had rammed the wedding through, deleted all the groom's friends off the guest list, and demanded they move to a larger home right away. Testimony about her later kicking her husband to the curb when he lost his job might be relevant only if it shows she was similarly unsupportive of him from the beginning.

They may fear that someone will read what they wrote. You can reassure them that, for the most part, their testimony is confidential. There is a brief period in the annulment process where the couple and their advocates (no one else) may go to the tribunal offices and review all of the testimony from both sides and from any experts who have been called. They may not take notes or make copies. The number of those who make this effort, or even care, is very small. Still, there may be a legitimate fear of family recrimination. Ask your advocate to help.

They may throw a few "nice" but damaging things in to offset the bad. One witness shared stories of the groom's numerous sexual partners before, during, and after the wedding, and the bride's longstanding addiction to casinos and the huge debt she hid from her husband-to-be. But feeling bad about saying those things, she added, "Yes, they were mature enough to get married, knew what they were doing, and really loved each other. They were good Catholics." Sometimes witnesses who are not educated in or aware of deep psychological issues are not in a position to testify to actual maturity or readiness. That's when their testimony can simply be helpful in supporting the facts in the testimony of others, including the Petitioner and the Respondent.

What the witnesses say

The tribunal has no objection—as in civil courts—to what might be called hearsay or that which appears to lack relevancy to the case. The judges will study the testimony but it must be considered trustworthy and may not end up being valuable evidence.

Following up

Annulments may take up to a year or two in many areas, due to a number of factors, including shortage of staff. However, most tribunals report that the primary delays are due to an inability to gather evidence from witnesses.

The tribunal staff are not your personal secretaries, and it will be up to you—the Petitioner—to keep reminding your witnesses to complete their responses and send them to the tribunal. If one or more of your witnesses has delayed due to uncertainty on how to complete the questionnaire, you might have your advocate offer to call and help them with general questions.

Part 4

Receiving the Decision

Chapter 14

When You Get the Decision

What to do while waiting

PRAY. Don't make this the last thing you do. God wants to help you through this challenging time.

Check with the tribunal secretary every thirty to sixty days—not every week. Let them do their work.

Make a list of the *healing benefits* that have occurred and the *virtues* you may have developed since this process began.

Healing benefits

⬦ The catharsis of writing your story
⬦ The healing of having your story heard and believed by others
⬦ The trust and intimacy developed between you and your advocate
⬦ A deeper understanding of yourself and others
⬦ Compassion for yourself and others

◇ A deeper understanding of and love for the
  Church
◇ An effort to forgive all those who have
  hurt you
◇ Seeking forgiveness for your own failings
◇ A more mature understanding and active
  practice of the faith
◇ A return to the reception of the Sacraments

Virtues

◇ Courage to reopen painful old wounds and
  let them heal
◇ Courage to face fears about the past and the
  future
◇ Humility in admitting fault
◇ Humility in allowing the majority of blame
  to fall on you rather than pointing the fin-
  ger at the other person
◇ Humility and obedience in submitting your
  marriage to examination by the Church
◇ Deeper love for God, the Church, and
  others

*When you receive an affirmative decision (mar-
riage is proved to be invalid)*

If you have received an affirmative decision, first
thank God. Then thank your advocate, your pastor, and

anyone else who gave you help. You might send a thank-you note to the tribunal. They usually hear complaints and rarely get thanks.

An affirmative decision can be extremely painful for the Respondent. I have a close friend who married a beautiful woman with an ugly cocaine habit. He naively thought the love and stability he could offer would change her. She would be okay for months at a time, and they eventually had two beautiful little daughters. But every once in a while, she'd fall in with "bad company" and start using again. One night he got a call from the local police to come and get her. She was face down in her own vomit in a posh hotel where she had been prostituting herself for drugs. He did not want to give up on her and worked hard at enduring the misery to "save the marriage." He'd taken his vows seriously and believed God's grace could change her. But when she left, divorced him, and filed for annulment, he was angry that the Church could say "there was no marriage." In his mind and heart, there was. He left the Church.

Both the beauty and the risk of marriage is the mutuality that must be present.

The TRUTH can set you free . . . but the truth can also hurt.

It's sometimes difficult to remember that marriage is not brought about by the consent of just one person.

When you receive a vetitum

The tribunal judge may have assessed that you may not yet be ready to enter into a subsequent marriage, and as part of their pastoral (caring) efforts will issue a "vetitum." A vetitum is a provision in the decision of the tribunal requiring some action (almost always appropriate counseling) before any cleric is authorized to witness at a future wedding or convalidation. Failure to comply makes the future wedding illicit but not invalid.

When you receive a negative decision (not enough evidence to declare invalidity)

St. Paul the Apostle tells us to thank God in all circumstances—even when we get bad news—knowing that God promises to bring great good from even the worst trials. A negative decision doesn't mean the marriage was valid; *it means that, for whatever reason, the proof necessary has not been sufficiently demonstrated.*

If you decide to appeal

You may appeal your case by first writing to the tribunal of the first court, where new testimony and/ or new grounds may be proposed. Some appeals go to Rome. The process is nuanced, and your advocate should be able to advise or guide you. If it can ever be proved that much of the testimony was untruthful or misleading, the case can be reopened. Any affirmative decision based on perjured testimony will be overturned.

Sometimes a case that has been initially denied can be reopened when there is the cooperation of an important witness that was not previously available.

Going to Communion

"Why can't I receive Communion? I'm a good person!"

Divorce does not automatically bar you from communion. If you are not remarried outside the Church and are in the state of grace, you may go to Communion.

Many people demand that the Church include them in everything, but they are so preoccupied with themselves, they forget two important things about the act of receiving the Body and Blood of Jesus Christ into one's own body:

> *(1) Any person who receives Holy Communion is opening their mind, heart, and body to the sacramental presence of the Second Person of the Holy Trinity: Jesus Christ. And where Christ is, so always is the Father and the Spirit.*

Anyone who comes into such an intimate act with God should approach with deep reverence, genuine awe, and profound gratitude . . . not casually, demanding their rights, and stinking of serious sin. No person is to receive Holy Communion while he or she is in a state of serious sin. Sin still exists, and it can be a grievous offense to Our Lord. If we are open to receive Our God in Holy Communion with the unholy stench of serious sin, we are like the bride who goes to her wedding chamber unwashed, unkempt, and crusted with dirt. Gross . . . but true. Our Lord deserves the loving and humble gift of our cleanest, most sweet-smelling self. That's where the gift of the Sacrament of Reconciliation (Confession) is so effective.

> *Any person who receives Holy Communion is saying with their actions, both personally and publicly, "I am in communion with the Catholic Church and all that she teaches to be true (including the REAL PRESENCE of Jesus in the Eucharist) and by grace am living according to those teachings."*

Can you say that when you receive Communion? If you disagree with Church teachings and are not fully *in communion* with the Church, then you should not *go to Communion*. You also should not go to Communion if you believe the Eucharist is only a symbol. Holy Communion is not a right; it's a privilege.

How does this apply to a divorced person?

◇ Divorce itself is not a sin. If you are not civilly remarried, and not in a state of serious sin for any reason, you are free to

receive Our Lord in Holy (and intimate)
Communion.

◇ Some serious sin on your part may have
been involved in your divorce. If so, do not
approach the altar until you go to Confession and receive absolution, so that you may
approach Our Lord cleanly and sweetly.

◇ If you have civilly remarried prior to getting
an annulment, you are still presumed to be
married in the eyes of the Church and now
living in an illicit, invalid, and sinful second
union. Those seem to be harsh words, but
any way in which we "miss the mark" (root
meaning of sin) of being united with the
good and perfect will of God is *sinful*. It
kills grace in us. You would still be Catholic,
still be a member of the Church family, still
deeply loved by God . . . but nonetheless
you would not be in "full communion with"
the Church. You haven't publicly proved
your prior marriage's invalidity that would
free you to remarry. It's like you're driving
your car without a current and valid license.
Just as you are required not to drive the car
without the license and registration, you are
asked to refrain from Communion until you
get things in order *for the good of all*. No one
wants to keep you away from the Eucharist.

◇ If you are in the state of serious sin, or have remarried outside the church and do not have an annulment (yet), you may make a "spiritual communion" with Christ every day of the week—even minute if you want! He never stops inviting you to be in full communion with Him . . . *and His Church.* He and His Bride are one.

If you received a negative decision and don't remarry, you are still considered married, even though you may live as a single person. If you're in the state of grace, you may also receive the Sacraments because you remain in full communion with the Church.

However, if you have remarried outside the Church when one or both of you have a prior marriage that has not been declared null, you are in what is commonly called an "irregular" marriage. You are in the Church, but not in "full communion." Because your prior marriage(s) is presumed to be valid, you are publicly in a state of sin. Remember that sin is "missing the mark" and it cuts us off from the fullness of God's grace. There is a way to live that is much better for us and the Church wants us to know it and choose it.

Be prepared for how you may be treated

As you can see by now, the issues of marriage, divorce, and annulment are complex. The state of mind and much of what went on between a couple at the wedding and in the beginning of their marriage is generally not known to close friends and relatives, much less the general public. For that reason, when you divorce, others in the Church will be watching and may be even judging without the benefit of your private information. You can't always control that. But this can be an opportunity for you to develop the virtues of prudence (try not to discuss the situation with people who lack understanding) and patience (give the process and its resolution time).

Sadly, sometimes even a pastor who feels sympathetic for the struggles of a couple will want to sweep the hard issues under the rug in a well-meaning but misdirected effort to be pastoral. "You don't need to go through the annulment process," some pastors have said. Whether knowingly or unknowingly, that approach deprives the parties of the many benefits and virtues listed at the beginning of this chapter. This attempt at a "pastoral" quick-fix also tends to foster a sense of disobedience or disrespect for Church teachings.

It's easy to go to extremes in these matters. Some clergy or laity who do not understand can take a very hard line that often condemns the couple without knowing the fullness of truth: "You are still married to your ex-spouse, and you are living in sin with that woman you call your wife! How dare you show your face in church! You cannot receive the Eucharist, and you are not wanted here." They may as well add, "You can go to Hell!"

Others take what they call a more loving approach: "Oh, come on now! Jesus loves *everyone*. You are a good person, and clearly you two love each other. Your marriage is between you and God. Go ahead and do what you feel is best. Forget the hierarchy; we are the Church! The institutional Church has no business trying to tell you what to do in these matters." They may as well add, "The Church can go to Hell!"

There is some truth in *both* extremes.

Each case is different, and the truth will be found somewhere in the middle. We are called to seek the whole truth ... so help us God. Speaking the truth—as much as it may hurt—is always the most loving thing anyone can tell you. So be humble, obedient, and no matter what advice you get from others, or the decision you get from the tribunal, always seek the counsel of a wise and holy priest.

Redemptive suffering

Let's jump back to the beginning of this book, which reminds us that God is really the most important Person, that we were made for Him, and that His love is what will satisfy the longings in our heart. Earthly marriages will always give way to the Heavenly Marriage, and in this fallen world, justice will not always prevail. Only in Heaven will justice be brought to perfection.

In the meantime, we suffer.

Especially from divorce. And maybe even in the struggle to produce evidence of nullity to the tribunal.

But our suffering can have great meaning and power, as long as we don't waste it on anger and self-pity. The Church calls it "redemptive suffering." It works like this:

From the Cross, Jesus' suffering and death became the living fountain of all graces—including our salvation. That fountain of grace flows beyond time and space and is available for "drinking" for all time for every generation.

Your suffering also flows from you, like blood, and you can let it spill into the ground where it pools and coagulates, dries up, and does nothing . . . or you can (through an act of the will) unite your pain into the same river of redemption that flows from Jesus' side. The blood and water that flow from *your* heart can mingle with *His* and become a source of healing and grace for you and others.

In this way—by offering Him your suffering—He takes your pain and gives it the power of life. He uses your anguish to bring about greater good—even the salvation of souls.

Don't waste this precious "gift."

Chapter 15

A Word about Obedience

I SOMETIMES hear angry complaints from those out-side—or who have left—the Church, such as, "You Catholics don't think for yourselves. You're like dumb sheep who would walk right off a cliff if the Pope said so. For Pete's sake, *wake up!*"

Some think that Catholics are simply slaves to tradition, caught like fish in a net of rigid rituals, rules, and regulations. Well, these people really don't know what they are talking about, but in a sense they are on to something. Some in the Church do prefer the easy way; having their pastor simply tell them what to do and never having to grow in their understanding of the faith. They remain spiritual children because—let's face it—authentic Christianity is about Heaven and Hell, life and death, and going to a bloody cross. As John Eldredge says in his book, *Love and War,* our lives are a great love story set in a raging battle between good and evil. To be fully Catholic is a wild and dangerous way to live!

Those who want to keep it safe and sweet have not yet chosen to live the great adventure that is Christianity. Sadly, this is a grave irresponsibility that all but ignores the complex but rich treasures of the Catholic faith. But much of the time what looks like blind obedience to others is really the obedience of someone whose eyes have been opened. We know that Christ was always obedient to the Father, even unto death on a cross. We know that "responsible obedience"—knowing what you are choosing to obey and why—is not slavery but true freedom. Obedience is a virtuous fruit of humility and love of God. And in obedience to the Church, we are obedient to Christ.

Let me share a story I heard from Rowland.

Rowland had been married to Dolores for years, but I knew he had been married to and divorced from another woman when he was a young man. I was learning about annulments and was curious, so I asked, "Would you be willing to tell me the details of *your* annulment?"

He agreed and started where all annulments usually begin—at the beginning.

Rowland had been an only child whose parents were faithful Methodists. His mother taught Sunday School, and his father would read to him each night, either from Scripture or Rowland's other favorite, L. Frank Baum's *The Wizard of Oz*. When Rowland was eleven, he went with his parents to hear a popular Christian evangelist who deeply inspired him. When the preacher asked those who wanted to give their life to Christ to come up to the stage, Rowland stood. His parents were amazed and glad that their son walked up the aisle to the front of the room and publicly surrendered his heart to God that night.

But years later, one might hardly recognize the formerly devout boy who was now a young man caught up in the popular culture. As Catholics, we know that conversion is not a one-time event, but a continuing movement of the mind and heart to God. Rowland never left his Christian faith, but it sat on the shelf for many years. When he was in his early twenties, he began dating (and sleeping with) beautiful and vivacious Zora. After a while, all his friends began to marry, and Rowland automatically assumed this was the next logical step in his life, admitting to not having given much thought to the person he was about to marry.

"She was fun and sexy," Rowland told me. "That's what was important to me then. I made a big mistake."

Rowland shared that Zora did not *ever* want children. Rowland—who'd missed the joys of brothers and sisters in his own childhood—wanted to have a large family.

"Even before we married, she used birth control and it made me mad. I tried to convince her that we could afford children, but it made no difference. She told me she didn't want to ruin her figure with a pregnancy."

It became clear that Rowland had married Zora before being aware of some of her deep emotional issues.

"I even would try to get her drunk before we made love so she would forget her birth control. I tried every trick in the book, and sure enough, she did get pregnant."

"Wow!" I replied. "I know your motives were good, but that was pretty manipulative and disrespectful, don't you think?" I could talk to Rowland that way, and he agreed.

"Yes. Very. But I was young and headstrong . . . and selfish."

"What happened then?" I asked.

"She had an abortion without telling me. I found out later. In fact, a few years after that, she had another abortion, and that time I even drove her to the doctor. It's the one thing in my life I regret the most."

I was quiet as Rowland continued the story.

"After ten years, we finally got divorced. I didn't think God would want me to stay with a woman who kept killing our babies. There were probably others I never knew about."

"Then I met Dolores. She was beautiful, too, but the opposite of Zora. Where Zora was something of a party-girl, Dolores was educated and serious about life. She worked as a chemist for one of the large airline companies. We clicked right away and had long conversations about economics, politics, and religion. But Dolores was a cradle Catholic, and when she found out

I had been married and divorced, she said she could not marry me."

"That must have been a shock. What did you do then?" I asked.

"I told her that was ridiculous. She said I needed an annulment, and I knew nothing about that. I decided to set her straight and prove that the Catholic Church was not the 'one true Church of Christ' as she believed."

I listened as Rowland continued about how he embarked on a several-year study of the world's major religions, particularly Catholicism. He still saw Dolores on occasion. They lived in different states, but he sent her a dozen red roses every week for nearly four years while he dug deeply into Church teachings. He wasn't about to give up on her.

"Something very unexpected happened. The more I studied, the more I became convinced of the truth of the Catholic Church's teachings, especially on marriage. I'd asked God to keep me open to the truth during my search, and He did. I know Dolores was thrilled when I finally quit trying to challenge her faith and instead asked to be accepted into it. I was received into the Church and began going to Mass and receiving Communion with Dolores. Everyone was happy, including her family. We had hope, then, that I could petition for an annulment based on the fact that Zora had always refused children. Dolores accepted my proposal of marriage pending the outcome of the annulment. But what happened then made me nearly lose my faith."

"Keep going," I said. I was on the edge of my seat waiting to hear the rest of the story.

"I filed for a Decree of Nullity in my diocese on the grounds that Zora had permanently refused children. I cited our conversations before and after marriage and had several witnesses who heard some of those conversations. Zora even cooperated and admitted she'd always been against children—but she was afraid and ashamed to admit to the abortions. She'd remarried and was afraid her current husband would find out. It was a small town."

"Did other witnesses testify to her abortions?"

"No. They had known about them, but they were afraid. But I thought for sure with her testimony and mine, it would be clear. Then I waited for the decision. I found out later it was my advocate who screwed things up."

"What do you mean? You got a negative decision? *No way!* Why?"

Rowland told me that in the small town, in which very few priests worked in the tribunal, the advocate who had been assigned to the case (not his parish priest) was also acting as the defender of the bond—the one who is to uphold the indissolubility of the marriage bond.

"He wore two hats. How can you be impartial under those circumstances? I don't know how it ever happened, but he wrote the decision and cited that 'he who proves too much, proves little.'"

"What the heck does *that* mean?" I was angry hearing Rowland's story.

"Apparently the evidence was so overwhelmingly in my favor, he assumed I had paid off the witnesses or something. I confronted him, and we got into a huge argument. It was no use. He was in the power position. I wasn't."

I sat in silence and waited for Rowland to cool off a bit.

"Then I appealed to the second court, which was in a large, metropolitan city. But not before I read every canon law myself, and made sure I had a case. In my appeal I cited all the relevant canons and figured those big-city guys had it more together than my hayseed pastor."

I laughed out loud. I have the greatest respect for the priesthood, but I understood Rowland's angst.

"They turned me down. I found out later that the second court rarely overturns a decision and maybe there were some good-ol'-boys politics going on. I guess I'll never know."

"Okay. So you lost. What then?"

"Dolores and I consulted with our respective pastors. We truly believed that according to the clear teachings of the Church, my prior marriage had been invalid. *It just could not be proved in the local tribunal.* Our pastors had read most of the evidence and knew our story. They agreed we had been caught in an imperfectly implemented system."

"So obviously you married anyway. Then what?"

"Neither of us was about to give up the faith. We both loved God *and* His Church and refused to leave in a huff over some of the injustices that we'd experienced. You don't leave Peter because of Judas!"

I laughed again. The situation wasn't funny, but Rowland—an outspoken man who had colorful language and clever idioms—was.

"So, after a lot of prayer and the support of our pastor, we decide to get civilly married and continue to be as actively involved in our parish life as we could. We promised each other that if we had children—which I hoped for—we'd raise them in the Catholic faith and make sure they went to Catholic schools."

"But neither of you could receive the Sacraments anymore, right?"

"Right. It was a very difficult cross to bear. I had been so excited as a convert to learn about the Real Presence of Jesus and to receive Him in the Eucharist. I'd known the joys of the graces that came from a good confession. But no more. Dolores and I were obedient to the Church. We went to Mass every week and raised our nine children in the faith. Every time one of our children made his or her First Communion we were thrilled, but anguished at the same time. We confessed to God the best we could and Dolores taught me about 'spiritual communions.'"

Fifteen years went by as Rowland and Dolores lived their Catholic faith at home, in business, and the community. And not receiving the Sacraments.

One day their parish priest called and said, "Why don't you two come over for dinner tomorrow night. I have something I want to tell you and Dolores."

Rowland had been a general contractor and had helped to build the school and church. Dolores was active in the women's guild and school committees, so dinners with the parish priest were not uncommon. When they'd first moved to their current parish, Rowland and Dolores had told their pastor the details of their marriage history. He and other priests in their community had long sympathized with the couple's irregular situation.

The next night the couple arrived and sat down in the rectory living room, where everyone exchanged pleasantries and a few jokes over cocktails.

"I have some good news for you two," the pastor finally announced.

Then he told the couple how the day before, there had been an intense convocation of all the priests in the diocese, a meeting where they heard from a prominent moral theologian who had come from and carried the authority of Rome. Marriage had been the topic, and the parish priest had decided to introduce Rowland and

Dolores's case—as an anonymous couple—to the papal emissary for his judgment. At this time in the Church, the annulment process was being carefully studied and refined, and this was a permitted process for judging this particular case.

"Even though your identity was not revealed, nearly all the priests in the room knew I was talking about you two. We all know your story—we've baptized your children—and we all shared how your annulment had not been handled well. How you'd been faithful for almost sixteen years, and more particularly, responsibly obedient. The man listened carefully to us and after many questions, review of the documents, and long discussions, he acknowledged that the case was clear and injustice had been done. He ruled that *you could be returned to the Sacraments through a special dispensation.* Immediately."

Rowland and his wife were stunned.

"That means you can go to Communion with your nine children tomorrow at morning Mass."

Dolores started crying. Rowland got up and started to pour another drink.

"Wait a minute," the pastor said, laughing. "First things first."

Then he said soberly, "I think this is the time for me to hear your confessions."

He paused to let it all sink in. "Who wants to be first?"

Dolores started crying again.

That night, in the rectory kitchen, Rowland and Dolores took turns making their first confessions to their pastor after so many years of waiting. So many years of painful obedience. Afterward there were tears of joy, hugs, laughter, and more drinks—and Rowland even brought out an expensive Cuban cigar. They stayed late, coming home well after midnight. When the baby-sitter left, they were still so excited, they went into their daughters' bedroom and woke their eldest child to share the good news.

They woke *me.*

"Yeah, Dad," I said to Rowland. "I remember that. I was fifteen. You and Mom were so happy, and I could smell the liquor on your breath!"

We both laughed heartily, and I got up and hugged him.

"Thanks, Dad."

I'd already known the "rest of the story," but now I had the background.

Rowland and Dolores, my parents, had been strong and faithful witnesses to me, my siblings, and the whole Church. They refused to leave the Church angry when things did not work out the way they should have. Or going to another parish and demanding the Sacraments. My mom and dad had always taught us that thoughtful and responsible obedience to the Church was obedience to Christ.

My dad would often explain, "How do you think *Jesus* felt when he begged the Father in the Garden of Olives to let things work out differently? What could have been more unjust than to be handed over to your death without cause? Your mother and I have no reason to be bitter. We have every reason to be obedient."

I'll never forget their story, and I hope you won't either.

Mom and Dad, the emissary from Rome, and the priest who served as both advocate and defender of the bond, are nearly all dead now. But the message lives on. If you go through the annulment process and, after the decision has been handed down, you face what you truly believe to be an injustice—whether you are the Petitioner or Respondent—please remember:

God is in control; we are not.

The world is not perfect, but Heaven is.

Suffering can be a path to deep holiness.

Obedience is a virtue that will bless you and your whole family.

Give God time and see what happens.

Chapter 16

Closing the Final Chapter

Giving the gift of forgiveness

YOU WERE probably reminded from the questions in this book how much two people can end up hurting one another—even when they never meant to. If you have not already given it, forgiveness is the final gift you must give your ex-spouse after the annulment process. And it goes both ways. Forgiveness is a gift you give yourself as well as another person. It can free you from bitterness.

Forgiving your ex-spouse and everyone else involved

Make a list of everyone who hurt you in your divorce and take it to prayer. Ask God to help you make a firm act of the will to forgive them—even if you don't feel like it. Forgiveness is not a feeling; it's a free choice to be obedient to God's leading. We're pretty sure Jesus did not *feel* like forgiving those who spat in His face and maimed and mangled Him. But He did.

Sometimes going to a person and saying, "I forgive you" can be an act of arrogance and can worsen the relationship. Unless a person specifically asks for your forgiveness—at which time you can give it to him or her—it may be best to keep the forgiveness in your heart.

Seeking forgiveness for your own failings

Perhaps even more important, *God calls you to seek forgiveness from your ex-spouse* (and others) for all the ways in which you failed him or her from the very beginning. When our pride still stands in the way, that can be scary!

I hope you have learned a lot about yourself from digging deeply into the past. You are a fallen creature who is also deeply loved and being redeemed. That goes for your former spouse as well. You two are no different in that regard.

Remember the bottomless well of God's deep and abundant Divine Mercy. That should give you the courage and determination to pick up the phone, write that letter, or send that email that says, something like:

> *I don't want to bring up all the details of the past, as it's not really necessary. But God is reminding me of the ways I have hurt you and failed as a spouse, and I ask you to forgive me.*

Don't just say, "I'm sorry." Instead, invite your former spouse to be an active part of the healing process by choosing to grant you forgiveness.

Don't allow yourself to get sucked into an argument about details. The other person may not be ready for this conversation, and that is okay. Repeat your request but then end it to avoid any further wounding.

Keep praying and maybe try again next year.

If your former spouse has died or you can't locate him or her, write a letter of apology or forgiveness and give it to you Spiritual Director, pastor, or a good friend.

Seek forgiveness from God

Now that you've made what Catholics call an "examination of conscience," and what those in twelve-step programs call a "searching and fearless moral inventory," take these burdens to God in the Sacrament of Penance (Confession).

Remember, you are not just going to the priest; you are going to Jesus Himself. That's what Sacraments are: intimate, loving encounters with God. He loves you and wants to heal the hurt from your divorce. Don't stay away from His tender mercies.

Considering a new marriage

Remember that little red valise that Cheryl brought to her honeymoon suite? Unless you go through the process of forgiving others—and seeking forgiveness from God and others—you will be carrying around festering wounds, unhealed fears, and a whole lot of stinking pride. Yuck. Who wants to marry someone like that? And all those character defects you had to face in telling your story? Do the loving thing and go get some help.

Part of the process of preparing for a new marriage is making sure you have the best you can offer someone else for a lifetime.

Take your time.

Learn how to enter dating and courtship the right way.

Grow close to Our Lord, and let Mary lead you to Him if you're hesitant.

May God bless you.

Frequently Asked Questions about Marriage and Annulment

THERE is a lot to know about marriage, divorce, and annulments—more than could ever fit into this book or even several volumes. But for a better understanding, this section is intended as a quick reference guide to some of the most common questions people ask about annulments.

A good use of this section might be when you are trying to explain annulments to your family or friends, or even your ex-spouse. Because annulments are about what may have gone wrong at the time a bride and groom said, "I do," we start first with an understanding of marriage.

What is marriage?

Marriage is one man and one woman living as husband and wife as instituted by God. It's both private and public, since whatever people do always affects the greater community. It has the power to bring the real presence of Christ into the union of husband and wife, in which He gives them the special graces necessary to have a loving and lasting marriage. But for Christ to be truly present, the relationship must be an image—and have the qualities—of His "marriage" to His Bride (all Christians). The Old Testament prophets and St. Paul in his letter to the Ephesians show that earthly marriage points to the "marriage" of God and mankind, Jesus and the Church. Christ's loving and permanent commitment to the Bride is freely chosen, never-ending, exclusive, faithful, and life-giving.

Can't anyone marry if they love each other?

No. Marriage by its very nature must mirror the life-giving union of Jesus and the Church or it will be something else, but not marriage. For earthly marriages to image and also get caught up into this heavenly marriage—and enjoy the graces that flow from it—there must be an exclusive (one man, one woman), permanent promise to live together in faithful love in a way that is open to life. Why? Jesus never deprives His Bride of His love or life, nor does the Bride close herself off from His life-giving love. Only a man and a woman who have the physiological identity for creating new life with God (procreating) or who do not purposely prevent procreation, can mirror this holy relationship. The couple must *intend* and *have the ability* to love the same way as Christ loves His Church: freely, fully, faithfully, and fruitfully.

What is a sacrament?

A sacrament is a holy way to enter into, and receive graces from, the sweetest act of love that Jesus—the Bridegroom—ever did for His Bride: *His suffering and death for her, overcoming sin for her, and His resurrection to new life, which she also enjoys.* Sacraments include earthly signs (persons, physical objects, and words of intent) that have the real power to make Jesus' real presence come into our lives to change us and give us new life.

Why is a sacrament so important?

Sacraments unite us with Christ in a way that is more intimate and more grace-filled than any other way we can be close to Him. They change us from the inside out. They fill us with God's love. They crucify our selfishness—our default sinful nature—and restore us to new spiritual life so we can love each other rightly. Who doesn't want *that* in their marriage?

When is marriage a sacrament?

Only baptized persons—who have received the life of the Holy Spirit—can enjoy the fullest graces of a sacrament. They can be Catholic or non-Catholic Christians. When both of the parties are baptized Christians, the marriage is presumed (unless proved otherwise) to be sacramental; that is, it can access the graces that flow from the "marriage" of Jesus and the Church.

When is a marriage non-sacramental?

Without Christian baptism, a person can't receive the fullness of graces that are available in a sacrament. Thus, without baptism, there is something missing that would cause the union to fully reflect the "marriage" of Jesus and His Bride. So a non-sacramental marriage occurs when there is at least one unbaptized party. This "good and natural" marriage can still enjoys God's blessings, but not the fullness of graces that flow from a sacrament.

Can non-baptized persons enjoy a good marriage?

Yes. God never withholds His love and grace from anyone who is open to it. Those who are unbaptized enjoy a "good and natural marriage," but they do not have the same fullness of graces available to them as those in a sacramental marriage.

When a Catholic marries, is it automatically sacramental?

No. Catholics are bound to marry within the Church in the manner that mirrors the marriage of Christ and His Bride. If they marry outside the Church, or in a way not prescribed by the Church, they invalidate their marriage. The Church calls this an "attempted" marriage, compassionately recognizing the desire of the couple to marry, but justly witnessing to the missing elements.

What is validity, and how is a marriage "valid"?

Just as states have certain requirements for civil marriage (e.g., a license, blood tests), the Church also has requirements before Catholics can be considered validly married. A valid Catholic marriage results from four elements: (1) the spouses are free to marry; (2) they are under no grave pressure or fear; (3) they intend to marry for life, to be completely faithful and be open to children; and (4) their consent is given in the presence of two witnesses and before a properly authorized Official Witness (minister). Exceptions to the last requirement must be approved by church authority. When these elements are present, the marriage mirrors the marriage between Christ and His Bride.

What is an attempted marriage?

It's when a couple says, "I do," but some essential element was missing that would result in an invalid marriage bond. The Church recognizes there may have been some good will and diligent effort, but it was an attempt at best.

What is an annulment?

Not to be confused with a civil annulment, it is the formal declaration of the Church that no valid marriage took place at the wedding, and the correct term is "Decree of Nullity." Despite heartfelt and good intentions, some people simply aren't able to live up to the vows they exchange, due perhaps to an addiction, severe immaturity, or some outside pressure, such as an out-of-wedlock pregnancy. Some have reserved the option of divorce even though they hope it never happens. These conditions may affect their consent ("I do") to the point that it is invalid. The church court (tribunal) investigates to see that what may have looked like a valid marriage was in fact not. Only with sufficient proof can the Church issue a Decree of Nullity, witnessing to and publicly declaring the bond invalid. It does not deny that a relationship ever existed or that the spouses love one another, nor does it make children illegitimate.

What could make a marriage bond invalid?

Consent makes the marriage; imperfect consent invalidates it. Consent is the act of the will to say, "I do," and it is affected by the *who, what, when, where,* and *why* of the bride and groom. The Church knows that some people just aren't capable of entering into marriage, as some children are not capable enough to drive a car, even though their feet reach the pedals and they really want to drive. And the church also recognizes—with the same love of justice and desire for mercy Jesus has—that despite good intent, best efforts, and maybe a very long time, something vital was missing or in the way that prevented the marriage bond from being valid.

What are some common things that could invalidate a marriage bond?

Maybe one spouse was married before and never received a Decree of Nullity. Or one was grossly immature, underage, under grave fear or pressure to marry (shotgun weddings), severely addicted, or not open to the gift of children. There are many reasons a union might not reflect the *free, full, faithful,* and *fruitful* love of the heavenly marriage of Jesus and His Bride.

How does the Church have the authority to declare a marriage invalid?

First, the Church is made up of all baptized Catholics who are in the Body of Christ and who are governed by the Pope, bishops, and priests by the authority passed down from Jesus through St. Peter. In relation to God, the Church is a "she"—the Bride of Christ, which is not just an analogy. She enjoys His love, protection against error, and she has been given His authority to teach, nurture, guide, protect, and govern her "children" so they can get to Heaven. In the annulment process, the Church has the authority from Jesus Himself to investigate a marriage to discover and uphold the truth. The Church has NO POWER to break an authentic marriage bond, but she does have the authority to determine—after thorough investigation—whether that bond was valid to begin with. Even if the parties wanted or hoped for a valid bond, maybe one or both of them did not have the capacity or full intent to live it. One example is when a bride or groom thinks, "Well, I hope we make it, but if he/she ever cheats on me, it's a deal breaker. I'm outta here!" In that case, the person has decided against the permanency of marriage. The person's outward "I do" is contradicted (invalidated) by his or her interior reservations. But that intent has to be proven.

How exactly does the Church issue a Decree of Nullity?

It's a thorough process that requires sometimes gut-wrenching honesty. The annulment process requires the skills of trained clergy and laity who takes a good, hard look at the situation—including detailed interviews and testimonies—and (to the best of human ability) brings generous doses of God's justice and mercy to the decision-making process. Those who worry that annulments are "too easily granted" can rest assured that the marriage bond is presumed valid until proven otherwise. And that usually takes a lot of proof.

What happens in the annulment process?

This is only a very brief overview:

⋄ An advocate will assist the Petitioner in presenting a Petition for Nullity.

- ◇ Both spouses must be given the opportunity to respond in detail and to present their case.
- ◇ Both bring in as many witnesses as necessary to corroborate their testimony.
- ◇ Both parties have the opportunity to read and review the other side's responses.
- ◇ The favor of the law goes to UPHOLDING THE MARRIAGE BOND.
- ◇ The burden of proof is on the one who says it was not valid.
- ◇ The Defender of the (Marriage) Bond is assigned to protect the indissolubility of the marriage and the rights of the responding party.
- ◇ The decision automatically goes to a second court for review.
- ◇ An appeal may be made in some cases.

How can a couple married twenty years—with three kids—get an annulment?

The annulment process examines the events leading up to, and at the time of, the wedding ceremony, to determine whether what was required for *a valid marriage bond* was ever brought about. While a marriage of twenty years shows that a couple had some capacity for a life-long commitment, the duration of their relationship in itself does not prove or negate the existence of the marriage bond at the time of "consent" (when they said, "I do"). Many people stay in invalid marriages for decades because of not wanting to abandon their children—which at its heart is a good thing! Some stay in invalid marriages for a long time for fear of shame, ridicule, being disowned, or of not being able to support themselves financially (in a manner they desire).

If a marriage is annulled, are the children from it considered illegitimate?

No. There is no effect on the legitimacy of children, since a child's mother and father were presumed to be married at the time that the child was born. Legitimacy is a concept that arose from the civil courts in response to establishing inheritance and protecting property. The Church has always recognized that every child is a unique and unrepeatable gift to the world, with great value and dignity that should be protected from conception to natural death.

How long does it take to get an annulment?

Some dioceses estimate a minimum of nine months and up to two years. The average time is reported to be about twelve to eighteen months to complete the entire process.

Why does it take so long?

We know a civil court case can extend for years. Similarly, it's easy to understand the complexity and depth of Canon (Church) Law and the investigative process in a Church annulment proceeding. The Petitioner must complete a lengthy questionnaire, and the Respondent and all the witnesses need sufficient time to prepare and submit their testimony. Documents such as baptism and marriage licenses must be acquired, sometimes from foreign countries, and submitted for review. All of the documentation needs to be analyzed by the tribunal, and when judgment is issued, everything goes to a second court for affirmation. Marriage and divorce are serious business and much is at stake, both privately and publicly. All this is done to protect the rights of all parties concerned and to uphold the indissolubility of a valid marriage bond.

Is there any way to speed up the process?

Yes and no. The most common delay in the process is the time required to secure witness testimony. The petitioner must ensure that the witnesses understand the importance of their participation and check with them frequently. Witnesses may be confused, hesitant, or have no sense of urgency in this matter. It will be up to the Petitioner to keep their response timely. After that, the process must take its course.

How much does it cost?

A fee (it may be between $200 and $1,000) is charged to cover diocesan administrative costs and can be made in payments. But the process is never denied or slowed because of an inability to pay. There may be other costs if expert witnesses (medical or psychological) need to be called in. Contrary to common myth, you can't "buy" an annulment.

Can I still go to Communion if I am divorced?

Yes, as long as you are not remarried outside the church or in the state of some other serious sin. Looking through the lens of the marriage analogy (with Christ as our Bridegroom and we as the Bride), we should never present ourselves bodily to Him in the Eucharist—an intimate act of "communion"—when we have the stench of serious, unconfessed sin. We need to "clean up" first. Being divorced is not a sin, but sinful behavior may have led up to it. You might need to go to Jesus in the Sacrament of Reconciliation (Confession) first. Don't make Him wait for you.

Can I remarry without an annulment and still receive Communion?

No. But this is not to punish you or keep you away from the Eucharist. If you have gone outside the Church and remarried, you are no longer in "full communion" with the Church. That may be able to be rectified, and the Church is here to help. Other people who are not in full communion with the Church—such as non-Catholics, or Catholics who publicly support abortion or reject Church teachings—are also required to refrain from receiving Communion, because they are not *in communion*. Their act of receiving Communion—whether public or private—would be a fraud.

Am I excommunicated from the Church if I am divorced?

No. Divorce can be the result of sin, but divorce does not put you outside the family of God. You are a valuable, loved member of the Body of Christ, and the Church wants to help you have the fullest means of grace in your life through the Sacraments.

If I get an annulment, am I free to remarry?

Maybe. Technically when you receive a Decree of Nullity for your former marriage(s), there is no valid bond that stands in the way of your entering another marriage. However, as this book explains, a valid marriage next time requires that you give consent in a way that reflects the bond between Christ and the Church. Your consent must be free of grave fear or pressure and open to children if you are still physically able to have them. You must have the mental and emotional maturity and capacity to say, "I do" to all that the Church requires of you, for your greatest good and holiness. That may require counseling and/or spiritual direction. The Church is here to help in that area, too, so talk to your pastor or other trusted Catholic leader.

What do I do when I receive the decision?

A faithful Catholic should obediently accept the authority of the Church tribunal as he or she would accept the decision of Christ. For Catholics, the answer is not about how we interpret laws, or how we feel; it's about surrendering in obedience to the authority Jesus gave His Bride, the Church—even when it seems unjust. It may seem a complicated cross to bear, *but not impossible with grace,* and one that can be spiritually fruitful. Obey the Church; trust God.

What if I feel I can't get an annulment?

Many people fear, resent, or fail to seek an annulment because they do not first have a full understanding of what it is. Maybe someone who didn't really know told you you'd never be able to get one. This is a complex situation but worthy of more research and an open mind. Please don't deprive yourself and others of a beautiful gift out of lack of knowledge and misunderstanding. *You might want to find an informed priest or a lay advocate who (1) has a sufficient understanding of* canon law, and (2) is faithful to the Church's teachings, and seek his or her counsel.

I still feel married, and I don't want an annulment!

You don't have to get one. Each person must decide, but only after an honest and careful study of Church teachings, competent spiritual direction, an open mind, and a heart willing to be obedient, accepting, and without bitterness.

The Pope said the United States is giving too many annulments. What about that?

In a certain sense, he's right. The annulment process, like any attempt to bring truth and order into the world, can be misused. But many applications for annulments get rejected in the initial stages for lack of evidence. However, our current culture has produced some of the most immature, selfish, entitled, addicted, and depressed adults who married too soon or for the wrong reasons, or who were utterly incapable of living out a sacramental marriage. Perhaps it is not so much about the U.S. tribunals' being free with annulments as it is their recognizing the sad state of our culture and the need for grace.

Glossary of Terms

Advocate: A person who helps you present your annulment case before the diocesan tribunal

Annulment, Church: The inaccurate but commonly used term for "Decree of Nullity"

Annulment, civil: The formal state declaration that a legal marriage bond never existed

Bride and Groom: One adult man and one adult woman who give consent to marriage

Canon: A particular Church law

Canon Law: The universal laws that govern the Church

Capacity: The mental, emotional, or physical ability of a person to enter into marriage

Civil divorce: A decree by the state that acknowledges a legal marriage and then dissolves it

Civil marriage: Marriage recognized by the state but not necessarily by the Church; civil marriages between non-Catholics are presumed to be valid

Consent: The act of the will by the spouses to marry each other, free from fear or pressure

Convalidation: Commonly called "having your marriage blessed" but much more than a mere blessing; it's a rite that elevates an existing civil marriage to the level of a sacrament

Covenant: An unbreakable bond that is more than just a contract

Declaration of Nullity: Another term for Decree of Nullity

Decree of Nullity: The formal decision issued by a Church tribunal that a marriage bond was invalid

Defender of the Bond: A member of the tribunal who defends the indissolubility of sacramental marriage and the rights of the Respondent

Diocese: The churches/parishes within a geographical area governed by a bishop

Dissolution of marriage: A civil term for divorce; the Church cannot declare a valid marriage "dissolved"

External Forum: The public dimension of the church

Form (of marriage): The way and the words that are used in a proper Catholic wedding; together with physical "matter", form is an essential element of a sacrament

Grave Lack of: A serious deficiency that is not likely to be overcome

Grounds: The causes by which a marriage bond can be declared null

Impediment: Something that stands in the way of the marriage bond's being valid

Indissolubility: An inability to be broken or dissolved; A valid marriage bond cannot be dissolved since Christ will never break his loving, eternal covenant ("marriage") to the Church (His Bride)

Intent: The act of the will to enter into marriage

Invalid: Quality of an action that lacks legal force or renders it null

Ligamen: When there has been a prior marriage that invalidates the subsequent (attempted) marriage

Marriage: A social institution, authored by God, in which one man and one woman live intimately as husband and wife; can be natural or sacramental

Marriage vows: The spoken expression of consent; must include proper form

Marriage, Christian: A covenantal partnership (between one man and one woman) of the whole of life, ordered to the good of the spouses and the procreation/education of children; also called sacramental marriage

Marriage, heavenly: The loving, life-giving, and permanent union of God and all those who receive Him in love; earthly marriage is a sign of the heavenly marriage

Marriage, natural: The union of one man and one woman (neither of whom are baptized) and who enjoy God's blessings but do not receive the fullness of graces that flow from a sacrament; also called a "good and natural marriage"

Marriage, non-sacramental: Marriage in which at least one of the spouses is unbaptized. God can bless this union, but it does not enjoy the fullness of grace that flows from a sacrament

Marriage, sacramental: A Christian marriage that is an effective sign of Christ's presence in the world; also called Christian marriage; the couple's love is purified and fulfilled by God in a way different from in a natural marriage

Matter: The physical element of a sacrament that —together with proper form/words—brings about the intended results (effects)

Matter (of marriage): The person(s) who makes an essential element of the sacrament

Ministers of marriage: The bride and groom who confer (ad-minister) the sacrament upon each other; the priest or deacon is commonly referred to as "the minister" but is more appropriately the Church's Official Witness

Nullity: The quality of being empty or void; nothing there, even despite appearances to the contrary

Official Witness: The Church's designated representative who witnesses as the couple confer the sacrament of marriage upon each other

Parties: The divorced husband and wife who are now Petitioner and Respondent in the annulment case

Petition: The formal request made of the diocesan tribunal to investigate the validity of a marriage bond

Petitioner: The spouse who petitions the tribunal to declare the marriage bond invalid

Respondent: The spouse who was married to the Petitioner

Sacrament: A visible action that has invisible, spiritual effects; it unites us with the saving work of Christ (His ultimate act of love for His Bride)

Tribunal: An assembly of canon lawyers, judges, and others appointed by the bishop, which investigates and decides that the annulment has been filed and proved (or not proved) according to canon law

Valid: The quality of an action that effects (makes happen) what it intends. It may or may not have been legally permitted (licit or illicit), but it still produced the intended effects

Valid consent: A free *intent* and *ability* to enter marriage as the Church prescribes

Valid marriage bond: Created when a man and woman give valid consent

Validity: presumption of the stand that the Church makes in presuming every marriage bond to be valid unless and until proven otherwise

Acknowledgments

ANNULMENT is a sensitive subject, and this book required a team effort of those who have love for not only the law but the couples who may have done their very best to make a marriage.

A special thank you to the following:

Terri Triviso, my lay advocate teammate in working with couples in the annulment process. You are right; two heads *are* better than one.

Msgr. James C. Kidder, parish priest, advocate, and one who has also served as a Defender for the Bond for over forty-five years. Your red pen is deeply appreciated.

The men and women of the San Bernardino Diocesan Tribunal who made themselves available to take calls, answer questions, and offer their help.

> *Trust in the Lord with all your heart,*
> *And lean not on your own understanding.*
> *Acknowledge Him in all your ways.*
> *And He will direct your path.*
> —Proverbs 3:5-6

$\mathscr{A}$LSO AVAILABLE FROM ROSE SWEET . . .

You CAN rebuild after divorce—it just takes a blueprint!

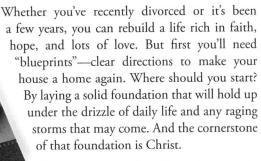

Whether you've recently divorced or it's been a few years, you can rebuild a life rich in faith, hope, and lots of love. But first you'll need "blueprints"—clear directions to make your house a home again. Where should you start? By laying a solid foundation that will hold up under the drizzle of daily life and any raging storms that may come. And the cornerstone of that foundation is Christ.

For over 20 years, Rose Sweet has brought her wit and wisdom to the separated, divorced, and remarried who often ask, "What is God's will for me?" "What about the kids?" "Where do I stand in the eyes of the Church?" or "Will I ever love again?" These and many other practical considerations are addressed in a way that will both challenge and encourage anyone who has been divorced.

I found myself falling into a cycle of depression and trying to fill my life with things—work, shopping, even hours of distraction on the computer. Rose reminded me what, or I should say Who, I really wanted. Now my life after divorce is not about finding friends on Facebook, but seeking the face of God. – Sharon

I knew God was with me, but wasn't sure about how to incorporate my faith into the daily details of my life. Rose helped me name and cut through my fears and showed me how to make it all work. – John

Price: $16.95
ISBN: 9781935302650

To order visit SAINTBENEDICTPRESS.COM or call 800.437.5876